DESIGNING WITH PLANTS

DESIGNING

WITH PLANTS

RICHARD L. AUSTIN, ASLA

VNR VAN NOSTRAND REINHOLD COMPANY
NEW YORK   CINCINNATI   TORONTO   LONDON   MELBOURNE

Copyright © 1982 by Van Nostrand Reinhold Company Inc.
Library of Congress Catalog Card Number 81-16490
ISBN 0-442-21056-6 (cloth)   0-442-24658-7 (paper)

Printed in the United States of America

Published by Van Nostrand Reinhold Company Inc.
135 West 50th Street, New York, NY 10020

Van Nostrand Reinhold Limited
1410 Birchmount Road
Scarborough, Ontario M1P 2E7, Canada

Van Nostrand Reinhold Australia Pty. Ltd.
17 Queen Street
Mitcham, Victoria 3132, Australia

Van Nostrand Reinhold Company Limited
Molly Millars Lane
Wokingham, Berkshire, England

16 15 14 13 12 11 10 9 8 7 6 5 4 3 2 1

Library of Congress Cataloging in Publication Data

Austin, Richard L.
    Designing with plants.

    Bibliography: p.
    Includes index.
    1. Landscape architecture.   I. Title.
SB472.A87   712   81-16490
ISBN 0-442-24658-7 (paper)   AACR2
ISBN 0-442-21056-6 (cloth)

ACKNOWLEDGMENTS

Various individuals have been generous in their willingness to help me with this work. For their invaluable contributions to the manuscript, I am indebted to Dr. Robert P. Ealy, Professor of Landscape Architecture and Mr. Dennis L. Law, Associate Professor of Landscape Architecture at Kansas State University.

The Foreword of this text was adapted from the original work, *Plants In Our Lives*, by Dr. Ealy. The narrative text to the graphics chapter was contributed by Mr. Law.

Portions of this book were developed by the author and Mr. Law for testing and refinement as a planting design text at the Department of Landscape Architecture, Kansas State University. It was originally developed as a handbook and appeared in print as *The Elements of Planting Design*.

Special thanks go to the individuals and firms that submitted plans, photographs, and sketches for use as illustrations in this text. They include Ms. Marge Edison, Landscape Architect, Manhattan, Kansas; Mr. Richard B. Myrick, Professor of Landscape Architecture, University of Texas at Arlington; Mr. Jerry L. Adamson, Landscape Architect, Omaha, Nebraska; and, Mr. Richard Sutton, Assistant Professor of Horticulture, University of Nebraska, Lincoln, Nebraska.

CONTENTS

FOREWORD

Plants have been with us from time immemorial. Just as mankind developed step by faltering step from ancient ancestors, so have the plants we know today struggled to survive the changing environment on our earth. Many of these plants were lost along the way while others, such as the Ginkgo, have survived without much modification. Most of them, however, have adapted to change and we see them today in a variety of forms.

When we think of the role of plants in our lives, each of us thinks of plants in relation to our own experiences. Probably the first thing that comes to mind for many of us is the plant origin of the food we eat. Perhaps for lunch we had fresh corn on the cob and a salad of lettuce and tomatoes, topped off with a slice of juicy watermelon for dessert. Even the animals we depend upon for our meat depend upon plants in the form of pasture grass, hay, or grain for nourishment.

In landscape design, we are often unaware of the visual impact that plants have upon us. In the autumn woods we note the bright colors of foliage and fruit displayed in great profusion; we listen to the sigh of the wind in the pines; we smell the smoke of a campfire. We see a distant mountaintop, white with a snowy crown. It contrasts with the blue of the autumn sky and the golden yellow of the dancing aspen leaves enframing the view. One can find a sense of well-being here—a peace of mind not present in the hurly-burly of our daily existence amid the cacophony of noises, smells, and sights of the city.

Landscape designers can use their knowledge, their "feel for nature," to bring some of the pleasantness of these autumn woods into our lives. They can look beneath the superficial and study the characteristics of plants, at what makes them appealing. The color value of plants is self-evident to many of us, yet some subtleties require a second look, a deeper perception. The red twigs of a dogwood shrub against the white of winter snow, the mottled bark of a sycamore or a true Chinese elm, and hundreds of other examples add up to many enjoyable experiences. We find color variations throughout the climatic seasons of the year—the fresh light green of new leaves in the spring, the variety of flower colors, the deeper green of summer foliage, the bright foliage colors of fall, and the delicate variations of winter twig and bark colors.

Texture is another characteristic that plants exhibit in great variety. Some are coarse, such as the Catalpa, with its large leaves, or the tropical banana plant. Others have medium-sized leaves or leaves that are small and narrow. This can also be a seasonal trait. Willows and other deciduous trees with small twigs produce a fine-textured effect when bare of leaves. On the other hand, the large twigs of the Kentucky

10

coffeebean or the tree of heaven give the viewer a coarser impression.

Plants come in all sorts of shapes and sizes. Form is a very important consideration of the landscape designer when choosing plants for a composition. People often recognize this characteristic more readily than any other, so it may be used more frequently to focus attention or to provide variety in a planting area. Grasses and creeping groundcovers give us low, spreading forms to provide living surfacing to many areas. Slightly higher are prostrate types such as Andorra creeping juniper and some of the cotoneasters. They are in turn exceeded by the round forms of Mugo pine and boxwoods, the vase shape of certain junipers, the towering pyramids of other narrow-leaved evergreens and sweet gums, the irregular asymmetry of Meyers juniper and selected firethorns, and the broad crowns of many deciduous shade trees. The list goes on and on, and the designer may use numerous varieties in a single composition.

The designer is often called upon to draw attention to a particular area. This can be done by focusing the view, through contrast, upon a plant or series of plants different from those nearby. For example, one ten-foot pyramidal green juniper among fifteen low-spreading green junipers would compel the viewer's attention through shape and size alone. Change it to a silver-gray Rocky Mountain juniper and you reinforce the accent of shape and size with color. Change the low plantings to low shrubs of contrasting texture and you have brought maximum contrast and accent into play.

In like manner we select plants to serve as background for objects such as a group of buildings viewed against a mountain slope or a piece of garden sculpture. If our goal is to focus upon an object, background plants must be subordinate to it. If they become more attractive to the viewer than the object, we have "missed the boat"; if they blend into a monotonous sameness of color, shape, and texture effect, we have failed again. If we select background plants that allow the object to dominate the view, we have accomplished our design goal.

There are many other related factors to be considered by the planting designer: defining space, reinforcing design, complementing architecture, framing good views, screening out undesirable views, controlling pedestrian movement, or providing interesting sound sources, seasonal changes, or shadow patterns for aesthetic effect. Plants professionally arranged along our major highways by landscape designers help reduce "highway hypnosis." Well-designed rest areas (roadside parks) also contribute to the safety of the auto driver, as do "crash control" plantings at selected spots.

The fact that plants have a psychological effect upon people should be understood by the landscape designer. Garrett Eckbo refers to plants as "our poetic lifeline back to Mother Nature in an increasingly denatured world."[1] The garden was the site where ancient Chinese philosophers contemplated man's role in the world. To many, plants may be symbolic of happenings in other times and places. To some the drooping branches of weeping willows suggest drooping spirits. The fragrance of spring flowers can lift our spirits, and the putrid smell of Gingko fruits can offend our nostrils. The sweating farmer, coming in from the summer wheat field, appreciates the shade of the cottonwoods near the house; these natural air conditioners fend off the rays of the sun and, through transpiration, add some evaporative, cooling effect to the area.

[1]Eckbo, Garrett, *The Landscape We See*, McGraw-Hill Book Company, New York, 1969, p. 141.

The landscape designer can use plants in several ways to modify the climate. Windbreaks and shelterbelts, and plantings for glare control and the control of soil moisture, drifting snow, and sinking cold air in a valley are all specific uses to which plants can be put. We know that plants, particularly trees and shrubs, serve as filters to screen out pollutant particles and also reduce irritating noises significantly.

During the Dust Bowl days of the 1930s, we became acutely aware of the need for using plantings to combat soil erosion. The Soil Conservation Service was organized to research the problem in consultation with other agencies and individuals. Improved tillage techniques for the soil surface were developed, as were plant uses to combat wind and rain erosion: windbreak and shelterbelt plantings of trees and shrubs, groundcover plantings of indigenous plant materials, dust- and sand-control plantings, grassed water channels, stream-bank stabilization, and watershed protection plantings.

Plants also serve as indicators, to the observant, of soil conditions. Sedges and cattails say "It is wet"; cacti and succulents say "It is dry." Ericaceous plants say "It is an acid soil"; saltgrass and atriplex say "It is salty here."

Certain plants produce symptoms that indicate the presence of air pollutants of various kinds. Grapes and redbud leaves become deformed, curled, cupped, and streaked with yellow when a chemical weed control, such as 2, 4-D, appears in the air. Tomato plants quickly succumb to gases such as methane, and dwarf Yaupon holly is quite susceptible to carbon monoxide from auto exhaust.

Many plants produce chemicals of value to the human race. The old herbalists knew of some of these many years ago. Native Americans used parts of the indigo bush,

Amorpha fruiticosa, as a dye and the crushed fruit as a means of stunning fish. We know now that the plant contains a chemical similar to rotenone, valuable as an insecticide; this latter chemical is derived from derris plants in Africa. In view of our concern about harmful chemical insecticides, we can instead use an organic insecticide that was known many years ago.

There are poisonous plants, too. From literature we have heard of hemlock. Our ranchers know the effect of loco weed on their cattle, and many of us have had firsthand experience with the irritation of poison ivy.

If we add the fact that perhaps a majority of us live in houses that are built in large part from lumber, we begin to see that mankind is highly dependent on plants. Much of the fuel we use for heat and energy may be directly or indirectly traced to plant origin. The very paper that this book is printed upon started out as wood pulp.

Last, but by no means least, plants provide a means of livelihood, completely or partially, for many people ranging from farmers to landscape designers.

Robert P. Ealy

DESIGNING WITH PLANTS

1/THE ECOLOGY OF PLANTING DESIGN

The common thread that links us, as landscape designers, to the environments we create is plant materials. Our repertoire of trees, shrubs, groundcovers, and grasses provides an extensive and complex base for selecting the ingredients that manipulate the spaces around us. We improve living conditions, protect the balance of wildlife, and prevent the deterioration of the environment with the proper placement of plants. It is important, therefore, to begin our coverage of design with the most important of considerations—the natural processes that control vegetation.

TYPES OF ECOLOGICAL SYSTEMS

Just as planting design relates to the profession of landscape architecture, landscape ecology provides the basic components of planting design. Solving intricate problems with plants requires an understanding of "how plants live, where they live,

17

and why they live where they do."[2] The selection, placement, and survival of each plant or plant mass depend upon the external forces that act upon them in a specific location. The two basic ecological systems for plants are the *individual system* and the *population system.*[2]

The *individual system* is genetically uniform wherever it occurs. Leaves, stems, and roots act as the total unit, and, under most circumstances, none of the parts can live without the others for very long. Some species generate vegetative parts (rhizomes or runners) that produce genetically identical plants (clones), but the parent plant still remains the individual with individual characteristics.

An individual plant relates to other plants in two ways: *genetically* to other members of the same species and *ecologically* to other plants in the community—forming a plant *population system*. When a population of plants becomes isolated and begins to inbreed with other groups, it is called a *local population*. It is from the local population in a specific environment that we begin to find genetic adaptation to the soil, climate, and water conditions. Certain genes or gene combinations begin to restrict the area in which the plant will grow and thrive. It is this restriction that is the key to selecting plants for a designed environment.

BIOLOGICAL AND PHYSICAL COMPONENTS

Individual plants and populations of species together form the total vegetative ecological system; this can range in size from a container of algae to a rain forest in South America. Although comprised of many interrelated parts, both biological components and physical components can be isolated.

The *biological components* consist of five relating energy levels. The first level is green vegetation, the part of the system that collects and stores energy from the sun. In storing this energy, the process of photosynthesis takes place, with a corresponding release of oxygen. The rest of the plant and animal communities are totally dependent upon this level. Green vegetation thus becomes the producer level for the ecological system.

The second level, the *herbivores*, ranges in size from a parasitic fungus to an elephant and is dependent upon the first level for its energy and food. Levels three and four are both comprised of *carnivores*—animals that eat herbivores. The lower form of carnivores, level three, relies exclusively on level two for energy. Level four, however, the higher form, may also get its energy from consuming members of level three. Man, the omnivore, eats both plants and animals. Level five is made up of bacteria, fungi, and protozoa—the *decomposers*—which use dead plants and animals for food and energy. This decayed matter in turn becomes an energy and food source for the green vegetation. Thus the chain of elements and events necessary for our existence on earth is completed (figure 1-1).

The ability of the *physical components* (living plants) to provide a specific design function is in part related to their hardiness and adaptability to local climate and microclimate conditions. Climate in this broad sense determines the types of plants that will grow in any given part of the world, but existing local conditions greatly modify the range of plants available to the designer. The range of plant types within the categories of broadleaf evergreens and narrowleaf evergreens is a good example. Narrowleaf plants generally will not survive the harsh summers of the broadleaf range. However, when the designer introduces more water with automatic sprinklers onto a site, or protects a plant from glaring sun and exposing dry winds, the microclimate is modified. This alteration of conditions extends a plant's design hardiness and adaptability.

The three most important physical components determin-

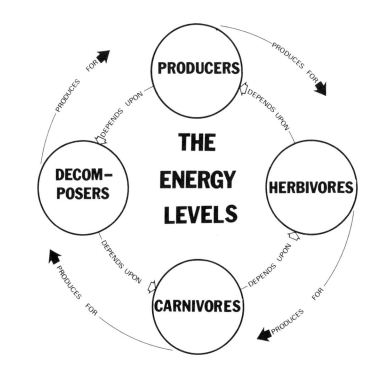

Figure 1-1. The five relating energy levels of the biological components.

ing adaptability and hardiness are: temperature (low/high and fluctuations), available water, and light.

Temperature determines plant growth; each plant has a minimum and a maximum temperature requirement. Temperature limits the distribution of plants and largely determines plant adaptability and hardiness in a particular region (figure 1-2). The limiting factors of temperature are:[1] short growing season; unfavorably high or low temperatures for proper development during growing season; harsh winter temperatures that injure or kill dormant plants; and temperatures favorable to the development of pest problems. Adaptability is generally related to the ability of the plant to enter a dormant or resting stage during which it is able to withstand widely variable temperature extremes. Many plants, especially deciduous woody plants, protect themselves by becoming dormant until temperatures are such that growth can occur again.

Water, both natural and supplemental, ranks next to temperature in determining plant distribution. Water may sometimes have a greater part to play in adaptability than in hardiness, but it is still important to the latter because plants under water stress may be more subject to low or high temperature injury. Plants are divided into three groups based upon their adaptability to moisture: *hydrophytes*, which are plants that will grow in water or on extremely wet sites; *mesophytes*, plants adapted to medium moisture conditions; and *xerophytes*, plants resistant to drought or extremely dry conditions. The ability of a plant to adapt to water extremes will largely determine its adaptability to a particular climate and design situation.

Energy, as *light*, falls to earth in the form of solar radiation and is the third key to the proliferation of plants. Light is energy that can be seen and is the main ingredient of photosynthesis.

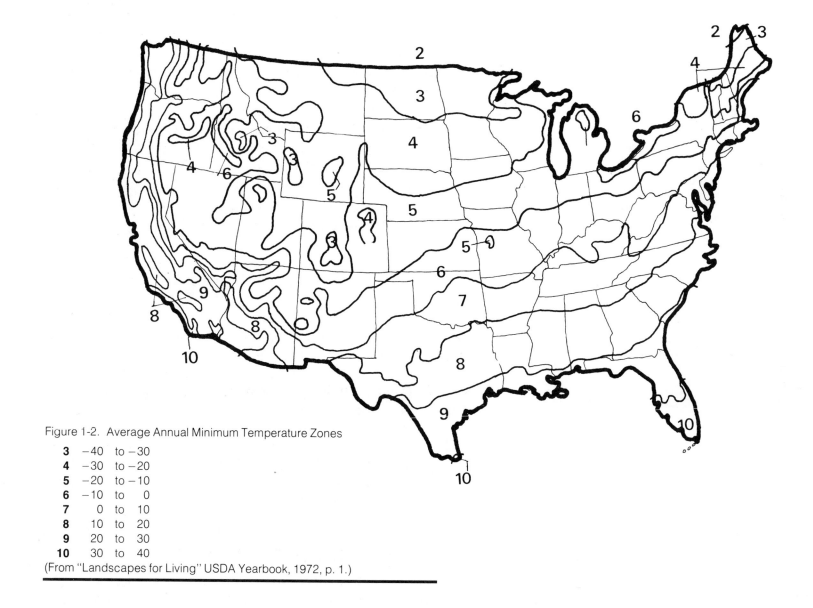

Figure 1-2. Average Annual Minimum Temperature Zones

3	−40	to	−30
4	−30	to	−20
5	−20	to	−10
6	−10	to	0
7	0	to	10
8	10	to	20
9	20	to	30
10	30	to	40

(From "Landscapes for Living" USDA Yearbook, 1972, p. 1.)

Light determines plant growth responses, but in many instances also relates to hardiness and adaptability. Exposure and temperature are interrelated, and both directly contribute to the ability of plants to adapt to local design or environmental conditions. The most important factors to consider for light are the placement of the plants and their exposure to sun or shade conditions.

When dealing with these factors and specific plants for a design, three aspects must be remembered:

1. *Intensity of light*, its brightness and its relationship to exposure requirements for planting. Some plant materials cannot withstand full sunlight while others cannot tolerate shade. The designer responds to this factor by filtering or increasing available light.
2. *Quality of the wavelength*, the relationship of the plant to ultraviolet (400 millimicrons) and/or infrared (760 millimicrons) light rays. The fact that a plant receives light does not necessarily mean that its requirements are being met, as some plants need more ultraviolet (blue light) than others. The designer adds or reduces this element to meet the needs of the materials chosen for a composition.
3. *Duration*, the length of time a plant may need to be exposed to light to produce flowers, seeds, or attractive foliage. If a small flowering tree or shrub remains in full sun only a short period of time during a day, the time needed to achieve full aesthetic quality may not be reached. The heavenly bamboo (*Nandina domestica*) needs infrared light to produce its attractive yellows and reds and, when placed in ultraviolet light, remains a cool green.

THE VEGETATIVE COMMUNITY

The community of organisms known broadly as plants is divided into four groups or subcommunities known as *divisions*:

1. *Thallophyta* (thallophytes) are non-chlorophyl-bearing with little or no woody structure, comprised of bacteria, lichens, and fungi.
2. *Bryophyta* (mosses and liverworts) are small green plants without flowers (in the popular sense).
3. *Pteridophyta* (ferns and fern allies) are green plants with vascular tissue, true roots, and a clear differentiation of leaf (frond) and stem; classes are true ferns, scouring rushes, club mosses, the tropical genus *Psilotum*, and quillworts.
4. *Spermatophyta* (seed plants) are distinct flowering plants having an embryo that germinates and are considered to be the most highly organized. The most distinct subdivisions are the gymnosperms (plants that produce a naked seek) and the angiosperms (plants that enclose the seed in an ovary).

THE LIFE FORMS OF PLANTS

It is important to understand the forms that a plant will take in its natural habitat. Nature has designed a unique relationship between plants and the environment, and this relationship is a key to their practical application in ornamental design.

The largest and most dominant is the *overstory tree* (the tallest of the natural forms, reaching a height of one hundred feet or more).[2,3] Next is the *understory tree* (a natural form that must have the overstory form above it in order to survive); since it depends upon the shade of the overstory, it has difficulty existing and adapting to conditions other than those of its natural habitat (figure 1-3). The *seedling tree* needs the protection of the understory to germinate and become a larger element of the natural environment. The *shrub* serves as a food and energy source for both animals and people, with herbs providing an additional protection for the soil. *Mosses* and *lichens* follow at the lower end of the life-form chain.

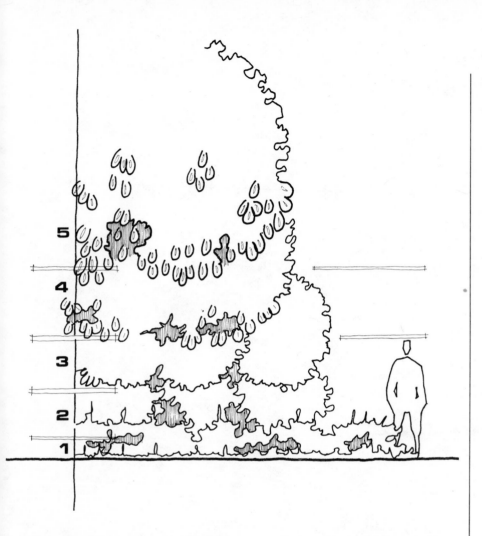

Figure 1-3. The life forms of plants as they occur in their natural habitat: (1) mosses and lichens; (2) shrub zone; (3) seedling tree zone; (4) understory zone; and (5) overstory zone.

MAJOR TYPES OF VEGETATION DEVELOPMENT

Successions have often been divided into primary and secondary. Primary successions begin in soilless areas that have not previously supported plants and animals; secondary successions, in areas with soil present.

Primary successions are divided into the following:

1. *Successions starting on relatively dry sites, such as rock outcroppings.* A characteristic sequence would start with lichens. As crevices become filled with fine particles of weathered rock, mosses and herbs would develop. Then a forest or grassland would follow, depending on the climatic conditions. Such successions take many centuries to many thousands of years before a continuous soil is produced from the rock outcroppings.

2. *Successions starting in ponds or lakes formed by such processes as glaciation.* Over thousands of years the pond becomes filled with the accumulation of dead plants. Algae and other submerged plants grow, die, and settle to the bottom, usually not decomposing as fast as they accumulate. As the bottom gets shallower, emergent plants such as bullrushes become established, followed by sedges and finally shrubs and trees when the peat soil builds up above the water level. Twenty, thirty, or forty feet of peat can accumulate in a few thousand years in a small lake or pond, and a forest will then grow in its place.

3. *Successions starting on ground-up rocks, such as glacial till.* Although ground-up rock is present, it is not a soil. It will not become soil until the rock particles chemically weather to free nutrients needed by plants and until humus (colloidal particles of organic matter) accumulates. These succes-

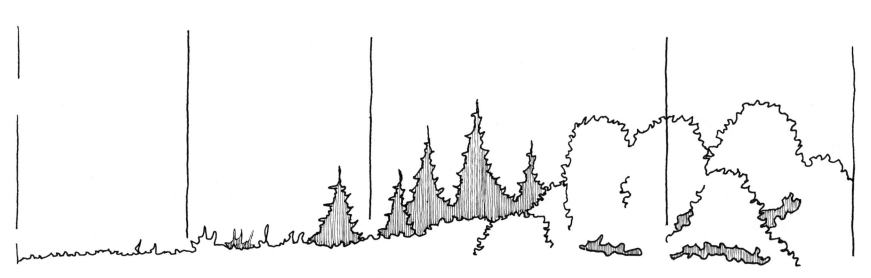

sions occur much faster than those starting in bedrock or ponds, but they are slower than secondary successions.

Secondary successions occur when a soil base is still present following a major disturbance that removes much or all the existing plant cover. Fire, heavy lumbering, and the abandonment of farm cultivation can result in the beginning of a secondary succession, provided that the soil remains stable (figure 1-4).

THE INDIVIDUAL PLANT AND ITS ENVIRONMENT

The distribution of a plant species depends upon the success or failure of individuals within the system. Processes found in each living organism determine not only the continuation of the species but also its use as a design element. A plant must do more than just survive—it must complete the reproductive cycle to become fully adaptable.[2,3]

Figure 1-4. Secondary succession is the most commonly encountered by the landscape designer.

Area 1—annual weeds, 1-5 years
Area 2—perennial grass, shrubs and young white pine, 3-20 years
Area 3—old white pine with young hardwoods underneath, 75-150 years
Area 4—self-replacing birch-beech-maple forest, 200 + years

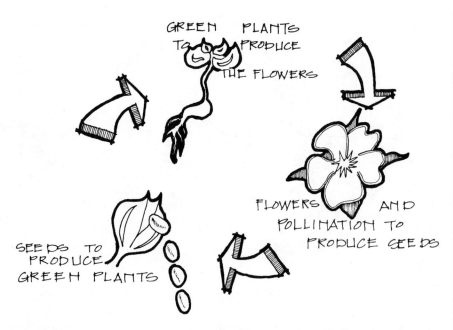

GREEN PLANTS TO PRODUCE THE FLOWERS

FLOWERS AND POLLINATION TO PRODUCE SEEDS

SEEDS TO PRODUCE GREEN PLANTS

Figure 1-5. The plant reproductive cycle is a process designed by nature.

The three stages in this cycle are *germination*, *vegetative growth*, and *flowering and fruiting*. Most plants, with the exception of ferns and mosses, start from seeds. The seed is a self-contained life unit relying upon moisture as the key factor for releasing the plant embryo (figure 1-5).

The germination of a seed is followed by vegetative growth—represented by the development of rootlets and sprouts. The roots start downward, following water and providing the anchor system of the plant. The roots will eventually have an outer covering similar to that of bark, with root hairs forming at the ends and near the drip line of the plant to assure moisture.

The stem system in the beginning pushes the seed leaves above the surface of the ground. Eventually it provides the terminal growing point (terminal bud) that concentrates the energy direction for the plant. Side buds (lateral growth) form, and soon the structure of the plant is permanently established. Another function of the stem system is the storage of food during dormancy periods. Some plants with weak aboveground systems (such as sweet potatoes and bulbs) have developed underground stems for storage.

For most plants above-ground development conditions their survival in the natural environment. The limbs grow and adjust as needed to expose the leaves to sunlight for the production of food. If, however, an environment becomes hostile to a plant's survival, evolutionary capabilities may emerge and allow the structure to adapt to extremes. Good examples of this are the groups of plants such as vines and creepers that have adapted to a clinging or twining habit for support. Their basic structure is such that other plant features give them their form.

Once the true leaves form, the plant becomes a complete

and productive organism. This structural element uses raw materials from the environment, converting and recycling ingredients into other reusable items—maintaining itself as one of the best-designed machines in nature (figure 1-6).

As a complete organism, the last stage in the process is flowering and fruiting. The flowers, regardless of their structural configuration, provide the link of seed fertilization by pollination. From fertilization the seeds develop, disperse, and germinate into a new plant—continuing the species (figure 1-7).[2]

GEOGRAPHIC DISTRIBUTION OF PLANTS

The existence and distribution of a plant in an ornamental setting or in a forest or open field is subject to the "approval" of the environment that surrounds it.[2]

There are two basic levels of distribution. *Macrodistribution* is geographic; plants at this level occur in a general region or pattern. *Microdistribution* is ecological, with species occurring only in certain kinds of environmental situations (i.e., north-facing slopes or the edges of streams and lakes).

A few species of plants are found almost everywhere and are referred to as *cosmopolitan species*. Others, with restricted distribution, are found in only one area and are called *endemic species*. Plants restricted to a given region (such as eastern North America) are *broad endemics* and include such plants as the flowering dogwood (*Cornus florida*) and ponderosa pine (*Pinus ponderosa*). Those restricted to the microenvironments in a narrow geographic area are *narrow endemics* and include the isolated redwoods (*Sequoia sempervirens*) of California.

The presence or absence of a winter season separates

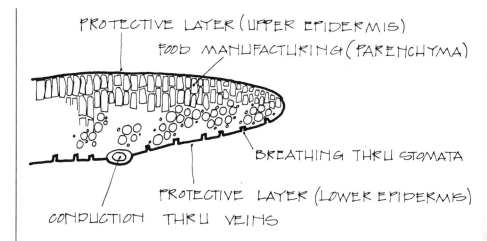

Figure 1-6. The leaf is the center of an extensive plant production system.

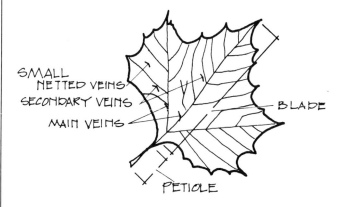

Figure 1-7.

the distribution of plants into three groups. The first, *arctic-alpine* (harsh winter), is made up primarily of perennial herbs occurring as tundra plants. The second, *temperate*, is made up of widely distributed species genetically capable of producing individuals adapted to different climates. The third, *pantropical*, consists of species located throughout the tropics in cultivated areas.[2]

TOLERANCE RANGES AND PRESENT DISTRIBUTIONS

In studying the distribution of plants in terms of their selection as design elements, the factor of tolerance range will be one of the most important considerations. The *tolerance range* of an individual plant is that range of environmental conditions in which the plant can be grown and will reproduce (figure 1-8). The more the genetic variety in a plant species, the greater the tolerance range.[2]

Tolerance range differs from *ecological range* in that the latter comprises a set of circumstances in which a plant actually does grow. For example, a species of plants may be tolerant to the conditions in Colorado but may only grow in New Mexico. This difference may lead to the introduction of a species into a new but compatible area and allow an expansion of its design capabilities.[2,3] The ecological range of a plant is governed by its *geographic* or *physical range*; if a plant can travel to other areas, it has a *potential geographic* or *physical range*.[2]

Two important design factors result from the study of plant ecology.

The first is the fact that a plant is a systematic, well-designed machine using specific fuel resources for the pro-

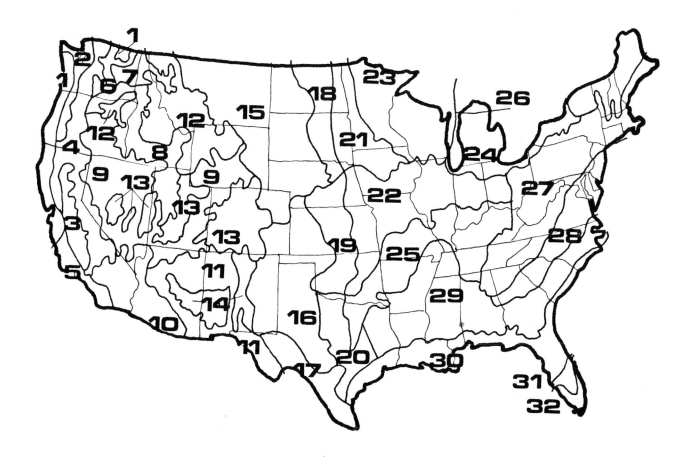

Figure 1-8. Plant Growth Regions of the United States:

1	North Pacific Coast	**12**	Northern Rocky Mountains	**23**	Western Great Lakes
2	Willamette Valley - Puget Sound	**13**	Central Rocky Mountains	**24**	Central Great Lakes
3	Central California Valleys	**14**	Southern Rocky Mountains	**25**	Ozark-Ohio-Tennessee River Valleys
4	Cascade Sierra Nevada	**15**	Northern Great Plains	**26**	Northern Great Lakes - St. Lawrence
5	Southern California	**16**	Central Great Plains	**27**	Appalachian
6	Columbia River Valley	**17**	Southern Plains	**28**	Piedmont
7	Palouse-Bitteroot Valley	**18**	Northern Black Soils	**29**	Upper Coastal Plain
8	Snake River Plain - Utah Valley	**19**	Central Black Soils	**30**	Swampy Coastal Plain
9	Great Basin-Intermontane	**20**	Southern Black Soils	**31**	South-Central Florida
10	Southwestern Desert	**21**	Northern Prairies	**32**	Subtropical Florida
11	Southern Plateau	**22**	Central Prairies		

(From "Landscapes for Living" USDA Yearbook, 1972, P. 178.)

duction of energy. These fuel resources (light, soil, water, and climate) are converted into the elements that sustain life on earth. Interruption or modification of the fuel that a plant needs results in the termination of the functional machine. A planting designer thus becomes a fuel supplier—creating the conditions within which a plant can live, produce, and reproduce.

The second factor is the relationship a plant has to various processes: the energy-producing process, the germination process, and the reproductive process. The systems of the plant world rely unquestionably upon *process*. The designed environment, in which the plant becomes the dominant architectural feature, should therefore be conditioned by it.

REFERENCES

[1]Austin, Richard L. and Dennis L. Law, *The Elements of Planting Design*, Interiors/Exteriors Publishing, Manhattan, Kansas, 1975.
[2]Billings, W. D., *Plants, Man and the Ecosystem*, Wadsworth Publishing Company, Belmont, California, 1970.
[3]Greenwood, Ned and J. M. B. Edwards, *Human Environments and Natural Systems*, Duxbury Press, Belmont, California, 1973.

2/ANALYSIS

A PROCESS FOR PLANTING DESIGN

In developing a planting composition, the landscape designer pursues a comprehensive solution to a series of related issues that result from the needs and desires of a client or client group. The final outcome should correlate design objectives with site limitations and provide a harmonious living environment.

As wood is to a carpenter or paint to a painter, the living growing plant is a basic medium to the landscape designer. Unlike other artists or plant professionals, the issues of "design function" must be considered before material selection and placement can be completed. Without the determination of function at the beginning of the planting-design process, the resulting composition will be nothing more than a disorganized arrangement of growing materials.

To facilitate an orderly and successful attainment of objectives in a planting design, a system of interviews, research, site considerations, and evaluations should be developed by a designer to assist in solving landscape problems. This comprehensive system should relate the importance of the original client needs and the issues of site limitations without eliminating the creative input of the designer. No process can be fully successful for a designer, however, without maintaining the major element of artistic ingression.

The following process includes the preplanning, design, and completion phases of a particular methodology. It is by no means an inclusive arrangement of steps and elements. Adjustments and modification may be necessary to relate the process to specific design abilities and site, energy, or budget limitations.

PHASE 1: PREPLANNING CONSIDERATIONS

This initial phase of the process should include the gathering of information pertinent to the design and planting of the envi-

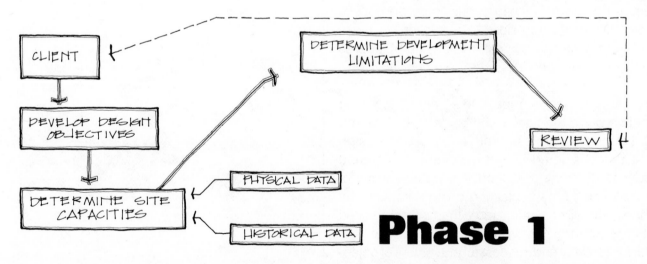

Figure 2-1.

ronment. The quality and extent of the information collected during this phase has a direct influence over the subsequent analysis and decision-making steps that follow. Care must be taken to collect information that is current and specifically related to the proposed environment.

STEP 1: DEVELOP DESIGN OBJECTIVES

The client or client group has very specific objectives in mind when a landscape development is contemplated. He, she, or they may want to develop a formal garden to support a sculpture exposition, for example, or enhance a corporate facility for employee rest and relaxation. Whatever the goals, the designer must first identify these issues and relate them in terms of design objectives or "design intent."

STEP 2: DEVELOP SITE CAPACITIES

The most honorable of goals may terminate abruptly if the site considered for development cannot support the desired objective. This important research step should examine the capability of the site to satisfy the intent. There are basically two areas to research: physical and historical information. Physical information can be divided into groups of property data and utility data. Historical information can be divided into abstracts (land-ownership documents that define the legal character of the property in question), easements (portions of the site upon which others may legally pass), and data of historical significance (historic sites or objects needing preservation).

The following outline will summarize the research that is needed:

I. Physical Information
   A. Property Data
      1. Topographic map: the contour lines of existing slopes and site features that may influence the proposed project.

2. Boundary lines: the limits of the design project as well as the property lines of the client program are important factors of this research step.
3. Slope analysis: the percent and orientation of the slope on the site.
4. Hydrology: sources of water (natural or artificial) on the site.
5. Climate: temperature, rainfall, and humidity ranges and directions of seasonal winds.
6. Soils: surface and subsurface elements and their relationship to plant materials.
7. Existing plants: materials that complement or interfere with the projected goals of the project.
8. Adjacent structures: how these features relate to the projected intent.

B. Utility Data
1. Availability: sources of potential facilities serving the site.
2. Location on site: above and/or below ground.
3. Size and capacity: in relation to present and future needs of the project.

II. Historical Information
A. Abstracts: titles and land data that may have a bearing on the future use of the site.
B. Easements: development restrictions of the site area.
C. Historically significant data: past and present land usage, zoning growth, and restrictions and preservation requirements.

STEP 3: DETERMINE DEVELOPMENT LIMITATIONS

Given the design intent and site-capacity research, the designer should be able to set forth specific site-development limitations and suggest alternatives that would satisfy the goals and objectives of the project. Present these limitations to the client and suggest development strategies. Three alternatives can be envisaged at this step: (1) all of the client objectives can be satisfied by the site; (2) a portion of the objectives can be met with minor alterations in either the client program or the site features; (3) none of the objectives can be met without major and costly modifications of the program or the site features.

It is at this phase of the process that the designer and/or the client should determine whether or not the project should be continued or abandoned (figure 2-1).

PHASE 2: DEVELOPING A PRELIMINARY PLAN

This phase consists of the arrangement of basic design elements into a preliminary set of design concepts that will fulfill the intended program. With continued input from the client, the designer begins to formulate specific decision-making steps necessary to the development of the planting plan.

STEP 1: DETERMINE FUNCTIONAL REQUIREMENTS OF THE PLANT MATERIALS

Establish the spatial shape of the planned environment based on the functional requirements of the program intent. The basic architectural forms of the plant materials (walls, ceilings, floors, canopies, barriers, baffles, screens, and groundcovers) should be considered.

STEP 2: DEVELOP PRELIMINARY CONCEPTS

Using the planting design elements—color, form, texture, and the like—determine the features within the space. These features, or small-scale environments, supported by the elements and controlled by the sculptured macroenvironment, reflect your planting design concepts. (The procedures for determining steps 1 and 2 are expanded in chapter 3.)

STEP 3: SELECT PLANT MATERIALS

The plant selection process should now occur. If a specific element is needed, such as a frame for an attractive view, a specific plant should be selected to fulfill the specific need.

STEP 4: DEVELOP A PRELIMINARY PLAN

Summarize your research, reviews, and design concepts in a preliminary development plan. Review it with the client, modify if necessary, and obtain approval (figure 2-2).

PHASE 3: DEVELOPING THE FINAL PLAN

STEP 1: PREPARE THE FINAL PLAN

If all the alternatives have been discussed and considered and a preliminary plan has been completed by the designer or design team, develop the final plan based upon a summary of all the preceding steps. Client input should be continually

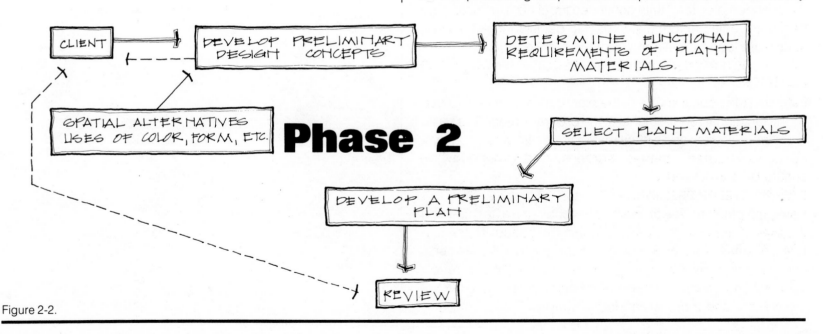

Figure 2-2.

36

maintained even though this is the final phase of the design process.

STEP 2: PREPARE SUPPORT AND IMPLEMENTATION DOCUMENTS

Develop the planting and construction details, installation and planting specifications, and maintenance requirements of the plan. The elements of your design may need to be communicated to a possible third party such as a government agency for approval. Make sure that you have presented all the necessary data.

STEP 3: PREPARE FOR IMPLEMENTATION

Develop the necessary documents to advertise the bidding process. Review and select the most comprehensive package to develop the planting design. Remember to review the steps to eliminate mistakes or evaluate alternatives (figure 2-3).

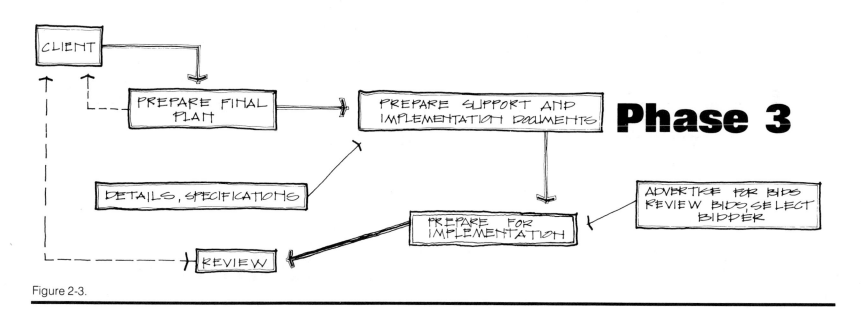

Figure 2-3.

PHASE 4: COMPLETION

STEP 1: IMPLEMENTATION/CONSTRUCTION
Although the basic design phases have been completed, installation may require changes to comply with unforeseen hazards at the site. Maintain a periodic review of the procedures selected and employed to achieve the design.

STEP 2: INSPECTION
During this final phase of the planting design process, inspect each area of the construction and provide for a final inspection to assure total compliance with the planting program.

STEP 3: EVALUATION
The plant material you have selected may be growing and prospering in their new home, but your function as a designer has not ended. As plants grow and mature, so does their relationship to the environment. Evaluate these changes and learn from mistakes of selection and judgment. Constant test-

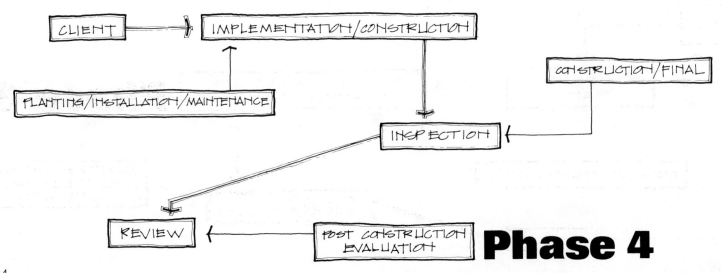

Figure 2-4.

ing of design results will make you a better planting designer (figure 2-4).

DEVELOPING DESIGN OBJECTIVES

The initial step in any process involves collecting information that will serve as a complete inventory of client needs and desires as well as the environmental characteristics of the proposed design space. From the client you should obtain specific information that will assist in identifying the "design intent"—the purpose of the planted space. It is in accordance with this intent that planting-design principles will be applied to develop the project.

The following questions should be directed to the client to identify the essential characteristics of the design:

How many persons will be using the space/site? What is the age/average age of these individuals?

What type of pedestrian access is needed to the space/site? Are there to be walks, ramps, or steps?

What type of vehicular access is needed to the site? Is there a need for off-street parking, delivery lanes, or emergency access?

How will the space/site be used? Is there a need to specify public areas, private areas, or service needs? Is the space/site to be used in a passive or an active manner?

(See Appendix 1 for a sample questionnaire to use when conducting an interview for a residential planting design.)

ANALYSIS CATEGORY DETERMINATION

The association of plants with a myriad of environmental factors requires intense and thorough preplanning investigations.

In most circumstances, the larger the project, the more involved the resource analysis becomes. With this in mind, the following identification of research factors may assist the planting designer.

TOPOGRAPHY/GRADES

Landform and structure play an important role in the location and placement of plant materials in a design. A complete understanding of this component is mandatory if special effects are desired for spatial environments within the landscaped area. Characteristics that should be noted include orientation of slope (north, south, east, west), because some plants need specific slope orientation to survive, and percentage of slope.

The *0 to 3*% topographic range is usually flat to gently sloping, but is subject to surface drainage problems. Soil depth for planting is greater in this range. Site modification is often less when accommodating structures and circulation facilities. If visual experiences are desired, the addition of large plant forms or berms will be needed.

The *3 to 8*% range is characterized by gently sloping to rolling terrain, offering a greater variety of interesting visual experiences. Soil often concentrates in low areas, and site-modification requirements for circulation and structures will increase.

In the *8 to 15*% range, hilly, often rocky terrain will expand the visual-experience potential of the site, but will also increase the costs of site modifications. Soil planting depths are too limited for an extensive introduction of ornamental plant materials.

The severe topographic problems occurring at the *15 to 25*% range make conventional development almost impossi-

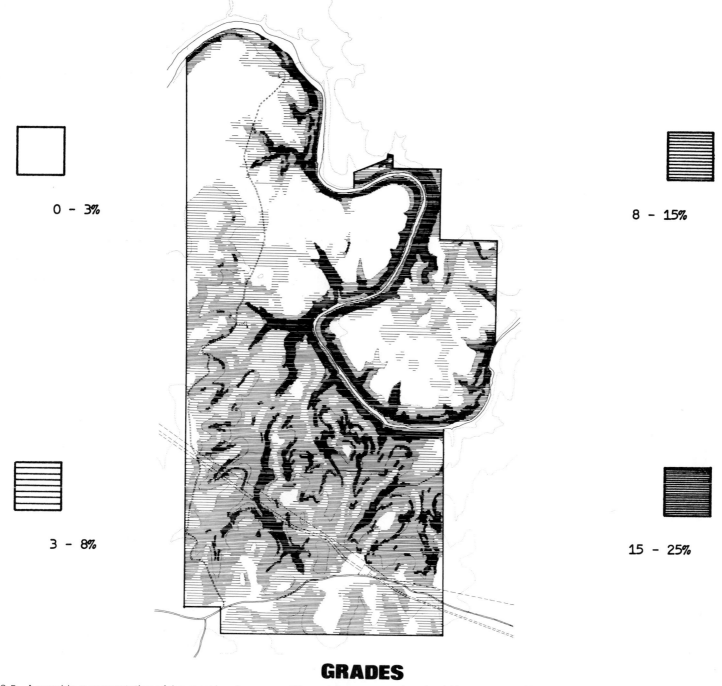

0 - 3%

8 - 15%

3 - 8%

15 - 25%

GRADES

Figure 2-5. A graphic representation of the most level areas and the most severe grades should be prepared. This illustration represents a large park project where topographic range will determine the final construction.

ble. Surface drainage is often dangerous and may require water retention or impoundment facilities. Short-distance visual experiences are easily created with plants and topography. Underground structures work well within this range.

VEGETATION

The location, size, condition, and potential for design should be determined for each plant or plant mass that exists on a site.

The *location* should be accurately marked on a base map, and the distance to other major features of the site recorded.

Vegetation *size* should be defined in terms of the width, length, and height of the material. For an individual tree, the caliper (the diameter of the trunk one foot above the ground) should be measured and recorded, and for a shrub the width at the base is important. The crown dimension (width of tree top) is referred to as the drip line and should be sketched on the plan for an individual plant as well as for a plant mass.

The *condition* of the plant or plant mass relates to its potential for continuous use. Storm, insect, or disease damage will limit its ability to satisfy its intended function. If obvious destruction is excessive, the designer will have to decide whether or not to repair or replace the material.

A plant's *potential for design* depends on the assessment of all the other factors. Design function is the criterion for determining if removal is necessary.

A review of the natural systems and conditions of the existing materials is important (*see* chapter 1). Existing vegetation is dependent on soil types, climates, and topography; as a separate component of design, the following should be recorded for evaluation:

1. *Existing vegetation.* If no plant material exists on the site, determine why. A designer must correct such conditions if possible.

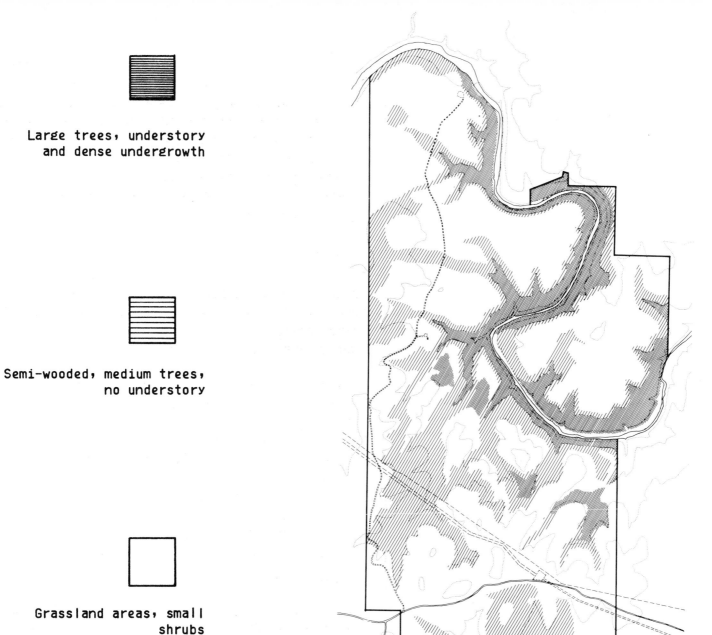

Large trees, understory
and dense undergrowth

Semi-wooded, medium trees,
no understory

Grassland areas, small
shrubs

VEGETATION

Figure 2-6. The vegetation on this site has been analyzed and assists the designer in selecting plants for use within the existing ecological systems.

2. *Successional stage of the plant materials.* Determine the stage of development of the existing plant materials. Does a *primary* or *secondary* successional condition exist? To what stage has it developed?
3. *Life-form characteristics.* Measure the density of the crown growth and the branching heights of both the understory and the overstory.

HYDROLOGY

Water is the key element to the success or failure of a planting composition. Using a plant or plants that require an unusual amount of water taxes the source of supply as well as the often limited patience of the client. Before beginning any planting operation, it is important to determine the following:

1. Exact location, size, and capacity of the source of water.
2. Quality of the water for the support of plant growth.
3. Potential costs for obtaining the water on the site.
4. Location of all sources of existing surface water such as lakes, ponds, and streams (these may be sources for irrigation).
5. Direction of the water flow and the extent of any watershed area (design should not interrupt natural flows).
6. Presence of sources of natural water such as springs, artesian wells, and streams (for natural planting areas).

CLIMATE

Overall temperatures and rainfall conditions will affect the outcome of the landscape environment created in a planting design. If the necessary conditions do not exist naturally, they will have to be supplied by the designer to provide the sources of fuel for the sustenance of the plant material. Although climate is intrinsically related to the other elements of analysis, specific data should be collected on the following:

    winds and breezes
        frequency during storm seasons
        prevailing directions, duration, seasons
    temperatures
        monthly averages, ranges
        extremes
        dates of killing frosts
    length of growing seasons
    sun angles
    precipitation
        annual and monthly rainfall
        annual and monthly snowfall
        humidity ranges

HISTORICAL ELEMENTS

The historical elements of any planting project are reflected specifically in the past uses of the site. Whether the proposed project site was previously a landfill, a chemical dump, an orchard, or a landscape nursery can have a profound effect on the success or failure of the design. Were there any historic structures that conditioned its use? Good sources for these research elements are the local historical societies or state historic agencies near the project site (figure 2-7).

SOILS

Planting design and soil are interrelated, as soil type may dictate planting design and design may in turn determine soil type or soil-modification requirements. Soil is basic to land-scaping and can occur in many different types, forms, and compositions.

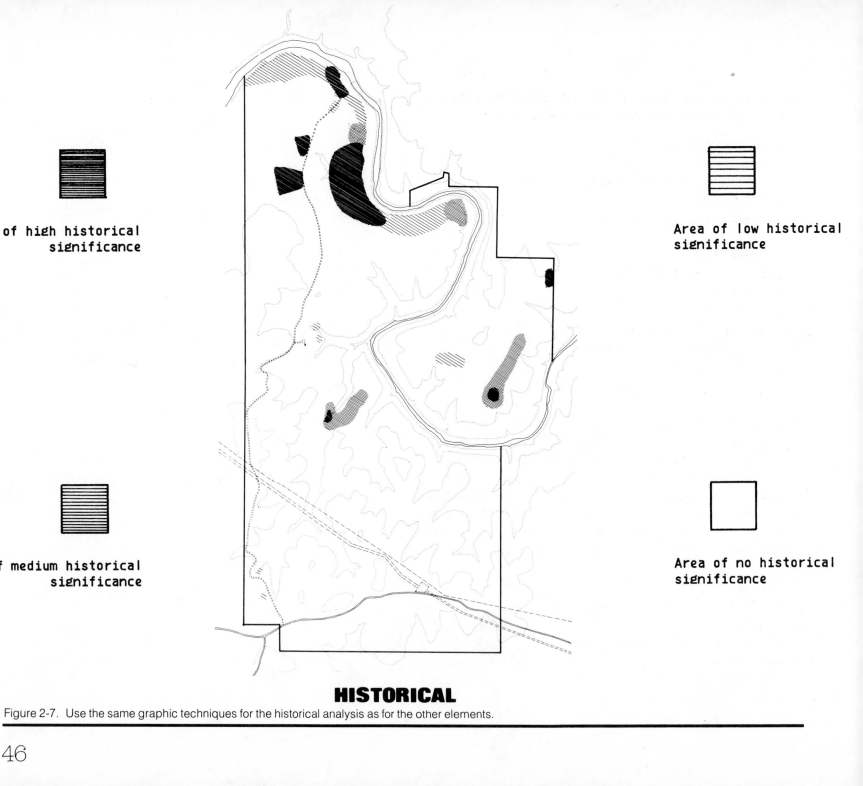

Area of high historical
significance

Area of low historical
significance

Area of medium historical
significance

Area of no historical
significance

HISTORICAL

Figure 2-7. Use the same graphic techniques for the historical analysis as for the other elements.

There are three soils that should be considered in planting design. Sand, loam, and clay comprise the three general planting types, with the percentage of their various components being the determining factor. A major component of any of these soils is the organic-matter content (O.M. content), which may vary from near zero to as high as 90 to 99%. In addition to O.M. content, the nutrient value may be a determining factor between a good soil and a poor soil (figure 2-8).

The planting designer is generally faced with a poor soil, consisting of a mixture of the local topsoil and varying amounts of subsoil, which often is mixed during the construction phases of the landscape development.

Critical to good planting is good soil, which can be defined as a mixture that has good structure and texture; is loose and friable; is high in organic and nutrient content; retains water but is also well drained and consequently high in oxygen content; and is of a proper pH to allow plant growth.

1. *Good structure and texture* measures the particles that make up a soil and how they are related to one another—in what percentages of sand, silt, and clay. A soil with more than 50% sand particles and correspondingly lesser percentages of silt and clay would obviously be classified as a sandy soil, but it could still be a good soil if the O.M. content were high enough to aid in water and nutrient retention.
2. *Good friability* refers to the ease of working within a range of moisture conditions. A heavy-clay soil, for example, is difficult to work when wet and impossible to work when dry.
3. *Good organic and nutrient content* aids in water retention, aeration, and binding nutrients.
4. *Adequate pH content* measures the acidity and alkalinity of a soil. In general, neutral or slightly acid soil is required for optimum growth of most plants.

Will support plant growth
without major reconstruction

Will support plant growth
with only minor reconstruction

Will not support plant growth
without major reconstruction

SOIL

Figure 2-8. A careful soils analysis will determine which soil amendments will be needed for planting.

Except under very unusual conditions, soil conditioning will be necessary prior to any planting operations, even for small-scale development. The following conditioning techniques are usually applied to improve the soil before planting:

1. addition of materials to correct mineral deficiencies (organic matter, chemical nutrients, alteration of pH) determined by soil test.
2. improvement of soil structure and texture by adding sand and organic matter to sand.
3. correction and control of water movement by providing proper subsurface drainage through subsoil modification via the addition of organic matter, a drain-tile system, or both.

SOIL ACIDITY

The underlying basis for plant growth is the intensity of the pH (potential of hydrogen ions), which may be rated on the following scale:

below 4.5	extremely acid
4.5 to 5.0	very strongly acid
5.1 to 5.5	strongly acid
5.6 to 6.0	medium acid
6.1 to 6.5	slightly acid
6.6 to 7.3	neutral
7.4 to 8.0	mildly alkaline
8.1 to 9.0	strongly alkaline
9.1 and above	very strongly alkaline

SOIL TYPES AND PLANT GROWTH

Light sandy loams are able to support a wide variety of plants for landscape use. Drainage of these soils is good. *Medium loams* are usually the best type because particles and drainage are balanced. *Heavy loams* are not as good as medium or light loams because of the need for extensive conditioning. *Clay* is usually too heavy for planting operations; drainage is unsatisfactory.

PLANT NUTRIENTS

Most soils are a derivative of geologic deposits and occur in layers. These layers, called *horizons*, provide the planting designer with a record of properties and growth capabilities of each soil type. The mineral properties of the soil are the most important factors to determine before planting and should include:

1. *Nitrogen*. The higher the organic-matter content the better the nitrogen availability, which is necessary for fertility. Excess nitrogen depresses the uptake of phosphorus and potassium. Inadequate nitrogen causes yellowing of foliage and weak plant growth.
2. *Phosphorus*. This is the essential element for growth and development. Too little of this material will obstruct the intake of other nutrients.
3. *Potassium*. Large quantities are needed for plant growth. An excess of this element reduces the uptake of magnesium.
4. *Calcium*. This element occurs more often in soil types with a high limestone content. It is useful as a soil conditioner rather than as a nutrient.
5. *Magnesium*. This is easily leached from light soils. A lack of this element may cause early defoliation.
6. *Iron*. High acidity helps break down this element for plants. Yellowing of leaves shows a lack of iron (iron chlorosis).
7. *Manganese*. Most peat and high-organic-content soils are

lacking in this element. A lack is characterized by a yellowing of leaves.

8. *Zinc and copper*. A lack of these elements results in weak plant growth and premature wilting.

To replenish a planting base deficient in any nutrient, the designer adds the various compounds either before, during, or after the planting process. Before planting, nutrients may be applied in mass to an entire site if necessary. During the actual planting process, the soil mix around the base of the plant may be supplemented. After planting, a periodic application of nutrients may be necessary to maintain plant quality.

Since most soil problems are best handled locally, a landscape designer should consult the Cooperative Extension Service, a part of the U.S. Department of Agriculture, for solutions to specific problems.

USING SOIL MAPS

The planting designer should consult the U.S. Department of Agriculture, Soil Conservation Service for current soil classification maps. Most of the research data needed for determining a design program can be obtained from these surveys.

WILDLIFE

An important, and often overlooked, factor in planting design is that of wildlife populations within the project area. How will the proposed design intent and planting operations relate to existing wildlife habitats? Some animal species are in danger of extinction primarily due to the loss of food sources. The planting designer can provide a valuable service with the introduction or protection of plant materials that will support and enhance the animals that may live within the spaces of the design area (figure 2-9).

Area of distinct
vegetative quality for
wildlife habitat
support

Area requiring
extensive improvement
for habitat support

Area of
vegetation needing
minimum improvement
for habitat
support

No major wildlife
habitat within this
area

WILDLIFE

Figure 2-9. Planting to support wildlife habitat is an important consideration in the analysis process.

Birds and small mammals—even rodents—will greatly expand the enjoyment of a designed space. The sounds of birds and the activities of other animals create experiences that cannot be achieved from any other source. The ecological support of a zoological garden cannot be achieved without correct selection and placement of plant materials by the landscape designer.

EXISTING CONDITIONS

The purpose of any analysis is to determine the existing land uses and conditions before design programs are initiated. The investigation of topography, vegetation, water, climate, history, soil, and wildlife should apply to any project. These individual ingredients, when blended in the decision-making process, serve to determine an environment's capacity to satisfy the intended needs of the people using the space. Without extensive preparation at the beginning, a landscape designer cannot make value judgments that will satisfy any project objectives.

3/DESIGN

COLOR

The color of a plant is the visual property that is dependent on the wavelength of the light reflected from it. It is the most striking of all the planting-design elements. It can attract attention to a plant or plant mass, influence the emotional effect caused by a landscape, create an atmosphere of warmth, produce a cooling effect, or add dignity or informality to a composition. Harmonious colors often produce satisfying designs even if structure is lacking. Careful attention should be directed to its selection.

The psychological effect of color is generally the same for most people, although color preference and impact vary among individuals. For example, bright colors tend to excite or stimulate, while subdued or cool colors are more conducive to restfulness and relaxation. Color is the result of a stimulus (light) reacting on the retina of the eye. This response is transmitted to the brain, which registers the stimulus—thus, color is seen. Each individual reacts to color in a personal way, and it is this response that gives originality to a landscape setting.

There are basically two types of color used by the designer in a planting composition. The first is background or *basic* color, used as a gentle wash to harmonize the view presented by the landscape. It should be pleasing and smooth to the eyes. The second is *accent* color, which is used to emphasize certain features of a composition. The use of color in planting design may be further classified into three types of compositions: *monochromatic*, using the same tone or color (green or brown) throughout the design; *complementary*, using washes of a dominant color with accents and mixtures of complementary colors; and *variegated,* using colors at random and painting a colorful picture with them.

The use of color and how it will appear to the person within a space are influenced by the distance at which it is viewed, the amount of direct or indirect light, the amount of shade, and the soil conditions of the planting area (figure 3-1).

Viewing distance is important if the full impact of a color is needed. Don't place important colors too far away from the viewer. Any color will become diffused by lights and shadows, creating an unwanted muddiness in the composition.

Direct or indirect light may often cause a plant color to dominate a composition and result in an unwanted glare. It may be necessary for a designer to diffuse the light reaching the plants by an overhead plant form or architectural feature.

Full or partial shade will soften or diffuse glaring colors and allow a greater range of experiences for the viewer.

Soil conditions will affect the colors of both plant foliage and flowers. The acidity level is the important factor and can be easily controlled mechanically.

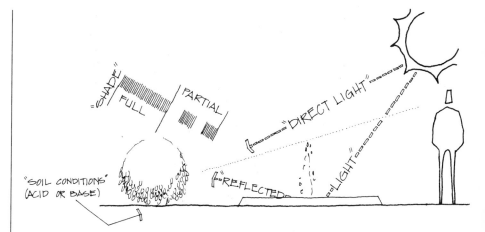

Figure 3-1. The viewing distance for a landscape plant is important if the full impact of the color element is to be considered in the design composition.

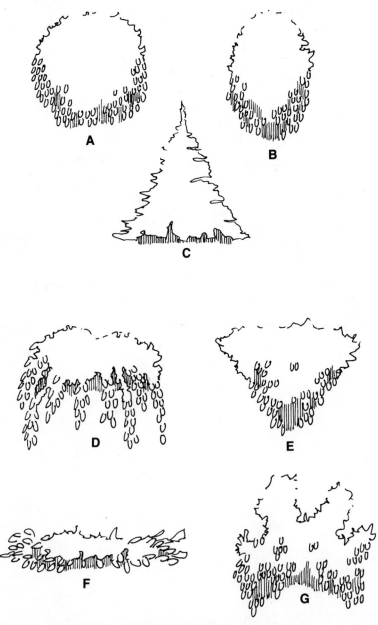

Figure 3-2. The general design terminology for plant materials is: (A) rounded or globular; (B) oval; (C) conical or pyramidal; (D) weeping or drooping; (E) upright; (F) spreading or horizontal; and, (G) irregular.

The following general principles should be remembered when using color in a composition:

People have a psychological tendency to lean toward light and vivid colors.

Subdued light and cool colors are more conducive to moody reflections of thought.

Bright light and warm colors tend to excite and may lead the viewer to move throughout a landscape space.

Each plant or plant mass must blend with its surroundings. Color changes should be gradated so as not to break continuity.

Warm colors such as reds, yellows, and oranges have a tendency to appear nearer to the observer or to advance, while cool colors such as blues and greens appear farther away or to recede.

Colors and textures are related in that delicate colors (tints and pastels) have a fine textural appearance, while harsher or brighter colors may imply a coarse texture.

FORM

Form involves the shape and structure of a plant or plant mass. It is used to indicate two-dimensional shapes (shapes that have only length and width) as well as three-dimensional shapes (those that have length, width, and thickness). Landscape designers, when completing a composition, think primarily in three-dimensional forms.

Every plant in the landscape has a distinct form that establishes its specific functional characteristics. General plant forms are rounded or globular, oval, conical or pyramidal, upright, weeping or drooping, spreading or horizontal, or irregular (figure 3-2).

The basic form of any plant depends upon an undisturbed habit of growth. If left alone, most plants reach their characteristic appearance at maturity, if not sooner. To alter the natural form of a plant and use a modified form in a composition, it is necessary to clip or shear the plant into the desired shape. A designer must remember, however, that such alteration procedures require excessive amounts of energy to develop and maintain. Continuous adjustments to the plant and the design may be necessary (figure 3-3).

Vertical forms can be used to create strong accents as well as to add height to a composition. Horizontal and spreading forms add width to tall structures. Weeping or drooping forms tend to create soft lines and also provide a tie to the ground plane. Rounded and globular forms are useful in creating large plant masses for borders and enclosures. These forms can be accented with contrasting shapes and/or contrasting materials to prevent monotony of composition (figure 3-4).

Plants that are similar in form always seem to belong together. They create harmonious planting compositions within themselves and with the group. The essential element of unification can be introduced into a planting design by using one dominant form throughout a composition (figure 3-5).

A variety of plant forms are used to create, define, enhance, and mold exterior spaces and to govern the way a viewer perceives the designed space. Two-dimensional form is flat and lacks depth. A three-dimensional convex form is experienced from without as the observer moves around to various vantage points. Three-dimensional concave form allows vantage points for visual experiences from within the design (figure 3-6).

Three-dimensional form is divided into two types: positive

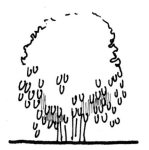

DECIDUOUS PLANTS ARE MORE ROUNDED . . . .

EVERGREEN TREES ARE MORE PYRAMIDAL . . . . .

EVERGREEN SHRUBS ARE MORE SPREADING . . . . .

Figure 3-3.

57

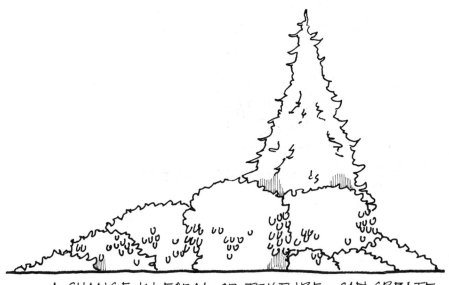

A CHANGE IN FORM OR TEXTURE CAN CREATE ACCENT

Figure 3-4.

and negative space. *Positive space* has a limited field of vision (enclosed) and is usually inner-focused. *Negative space* is the "leftover" space (open) and has an unlimited field of vision (figure 3-7).

In using form as a landscape-design element, the designer should go beyond the shape of an individual plant (single form) and use groups of plants (combined form) to accomplish the goals of a planting composition (figure 3-8). The choice of a dominant form will establish the overall character of the perceived exterior space and, when combined with the other design elements, determine the total quality of the plantings.

Figure 3-5. A tall, irregular form such as a tree will be accentuated when found in the midst of smooth stone.

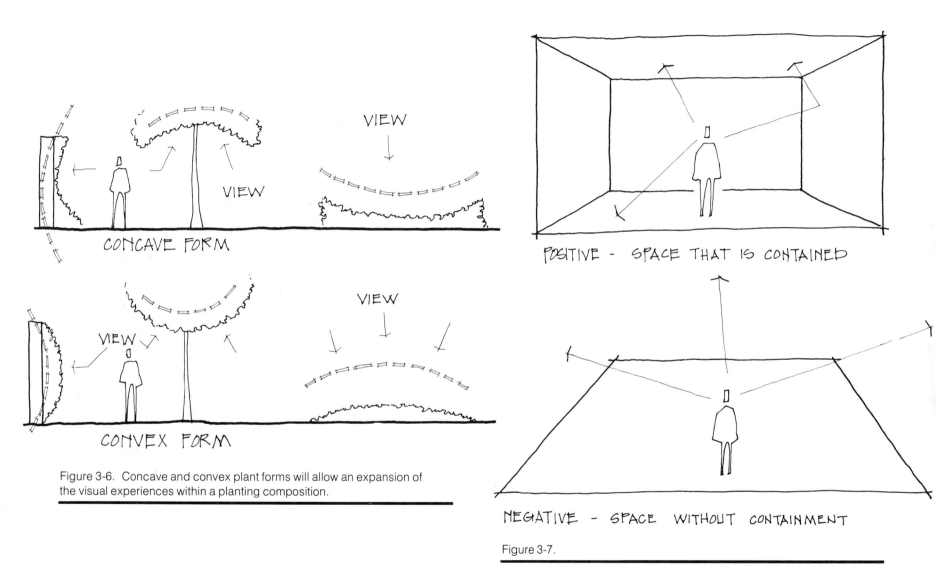

CONCAVE FORM

VIEW

VIEW

CONVEX FORM

VIEW

VIEW

Figure 3-6. Concave and convex plant forms will allow an expansion of the visual experiences within a planting composition.

POSITIVE - SPACE THAT IS CONTAINED

NEGATIVE - SPACE WITHOUT CONTAINMENT

Figure 3-7.

59

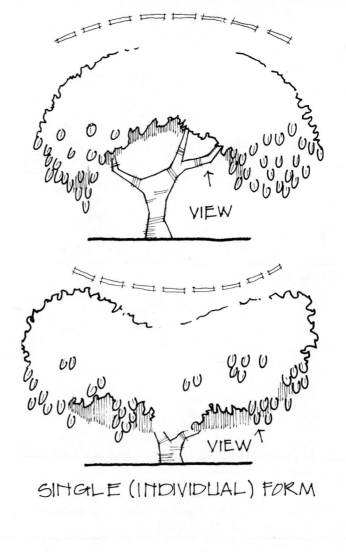

VIEW

SINGLE (INDIVIDUAL) FORM

SINGLE HORIZONTAL FORM

Figure 3-8. Both single plant forms and combined plant forms may be used to implement perceived spatial experiences.

REGULAR SPACING WILL MAINTAIN
INDIVIDUAL PLANT FORM

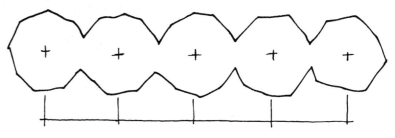

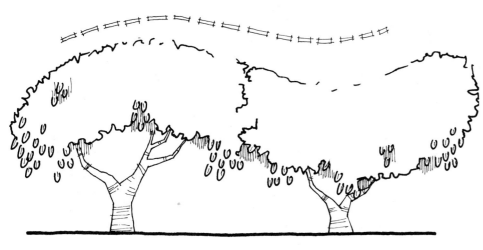

COMBINED (MASS) FORM

COMPRESSED SPACING WILL GIVE
A SPECIFIC FORM TO THE MASS

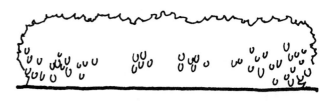

VIEW

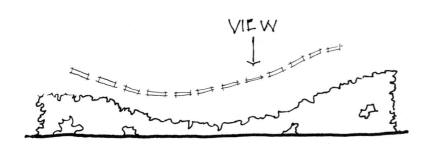

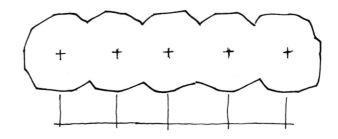

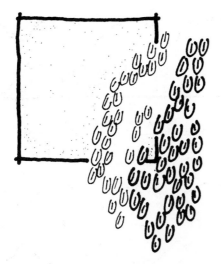

Figure 3-9.

TEXTURE

Texture is the surface quality of any plant material which can be seen or felt. It is a feature in planting design that is often overlooked and discounted as not being important. However, it provides the designer with an added dimension to give variety and interest to a planting composition. Texture can be interpreted as the tactile and visual character of the physical surface qualities as determined by the form, size, and aggregation of the units of which a plant is composed.

Texture should be considered in terms of comparison between plants in the design. A honey locust may have a somewhat fine texture when compared to a bur oak; but, when compared to a smooth stucco or concrete wall, it may appear rather coarse. Slender elm twigs have a lacy texture when compared to the stubby branches of oaks, and ferns have a more delicate visual texture than hackberries (figure 3-9).

Texture may also be qualified in terms of the distance from which the plant is viewed. The perceived size of the units varies with changes in distance. When we are close enough to touch an oak tree, we are able to see the form of the individual leaves and the texture of the leaf surfaces. At a distance of a hundred yards, we see the leaves only in the aggregate, not as individual units. Texture then becomes the entire mass.

In planting design, texture is the arrangement and size of leaves, twigs, or branches and is described by qualities of coarseness or fineness, roughness or smoothness, heaviness or lightness, thickness or thinness, which vary somewhat with the season of the year. The texture of a deciduous tree in winter is determined by the size, number, and position of its twigs and branches (thick or thin, numerous or sparse, congregated or scattered). When the tree is in leaf, its texture is primarily determined by the size, shape, number, and arrangement of leaves.

In the application of texture to planting design, each part of the plant must be so related that it blends with its neighbor. If textures change, they must do so in a logical and graduated manner. They should generally proceed in a sequence and not break continuity (figure 3-10).

Texture also has certain psychological and physical effects upon the viewer. For example, textures change in a sequence ranging from fine to medium to coarse or the reverse. A coarse-to-fine sequence can expand the composition, causing it to appear farther away, while a sequence from fine to coarse contracts the composition (figure 3-11). It must also be remembered that fine textures reflect more light from a given area than do coarse textures; this causes the fine textures to appear brighter. Glossy foliage reflects more light than does rough foliage and may cause the plant surface to alter in appearance.

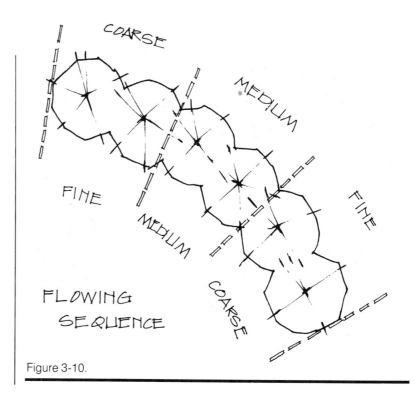

Figure 3-10.

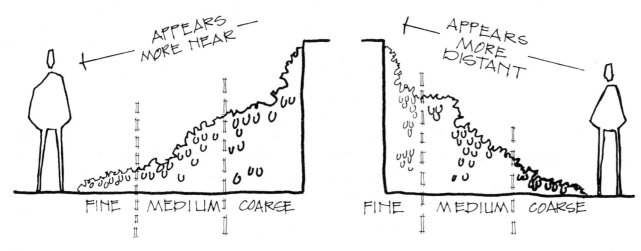

Figure 3-11.

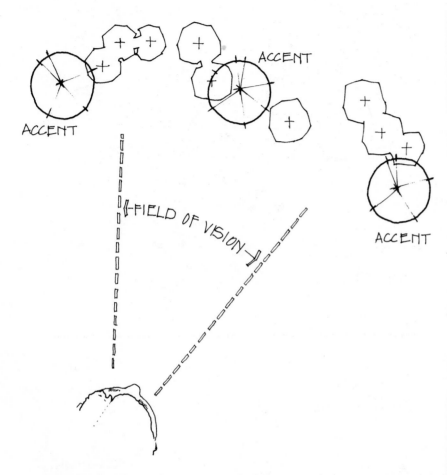

ACCENT

ACCENT

FIELD OF VISION

ACCENT

ACCENT

Figure 3-12. Only one accent feature should appear within the visual core of experience.

ACCENT

An accent is a visual break in a sequence or pattern of plant materials. It has a dramatic effect on the visual appearance of a landscaped environment by concentrating attention on a specific portion of the design and playing upon the natural perceptions of a viewer. Unlike other art forms, a landscape is usually viewed while walking through an exterior space, with attention varying from minute to minute with each step. The use of the accent element in a planting design can capture the attention of the viewer and control how the composition is seen.

For an accent to be effective, it must be strong. The human eye, with its ability to see peripherally, tends to wander aimlessly. With the use of strong accents, attention is demanded and captured (figure 3-12).

Be careful in the placement of accents within a given landscaped space. Too many accent points will cause confusion, which may repel the viewer.

In designing the exterior space, the location of focal points in the plan should revolve around areas of major activity.

If possible, the accent should be framed. This can be done by placing the point of emphasis in a "proper position" in relationship to the confines of a "window" or natural opening (figure 3-13).

Accent may also be created with texture. If the dominant plant pattern tends to have a fine texture, another plant with a medium or coarse texture will stand out as the accent feature.

A change in form will create a definite accent if one plant form is used predominantly but relieved by the introduction of a stronger, more dominant feature. This accent feature can be a plant of contrasting form, a piece of garden sculpture, or an architectural structure.

A contrast in the spacing of plants within the design composition will serve as a point of accent. Plant materials placed in a sequential order never attract until one of the units disappears (figure 3-14). This "gap" is eye-catching and will serve as a good planting-design accent. By varying the size of a certain object within a sequence, you can create a center of accent (figure 3-15).

The most vivid impact upon our senses is made by a color accent. In utilizing color, simply provide an abrupt color change in the plant-material sequences (figure 3-16).

Line can capture the eye and demand its attention. This can be accomplished through the use of lines that lead to or converge on a single point in the distance. With the use of plant walls or screens, vision can be physically limited to a focal point. This method is usually developed to enhance another accent (figures 3-17, 3-18).

Accent may be accomplished by grouping objects within a design composition. Plants of the same type should always be planted enmass in order to have a greater visual impact.

SCALE

Scale or proportion concerns the relationship of a plant to other plants and to the whole. When the relationship of one plant to another or of a group of plants to the total space is expressed in the human environment, the term *scale* is often used. In establishing scale within the landscape, the human subject is the standard. All aspects of the composition must be in scale with its users. There are several considerations that should be made in establishing scale.

First, scale is relative to the perception of the viewer. That perception may vary from individual to individual, but harmony

Figure 3-13. A "gap" in the spacing of tree trunks creates accent and draws the viewer's eye to the space beyond. The principle of *enframement* is indicated here with the tree trunk, lower limbs, and understory working together to frame the vista.

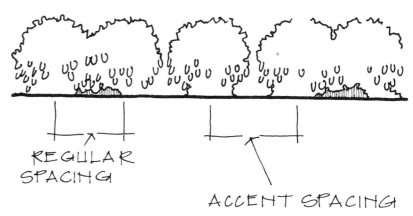

REGULAR SPACING

ACCENT SPACING

Figure 3-14. A spacing "gap" is eye-catching and will assist a designer in bringing attention to a mass of plant materials.

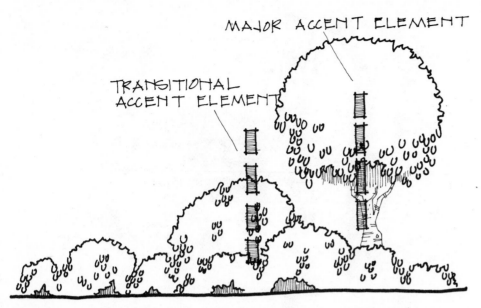

MAJOR ACCENT ELEMENT

TRANSITIONAL ACCENT ELEMENT

SIZE VARIATION IS AN IMPORTANT TOOL IN CREATING ACCENT...

A GRADUAL CHANGE IN SIZE CREATES A SOFT ACCENT

A SUDDEN CHANGE CREATES A MORE DRAMATIC ACCENT

Figure 3-15.

Figure 3-16. Color can be used to create definite accent within the landscape. This can be accomplished by the use of brightly colored annuals and perennials or by utilizing plant materials that produce colored foliage. White tree trunks against a dark background is also commonly used.

Figure 3-17. (*Facing page*) Plant materials are used here to support the architectural elements and to direct the attention of the viewer to the passageway. (Courtesy, Richard B. Myrick, Dallas, Texas)

Figure 3-18. Lines, supported by moving water, can demand attention and create *invitation*.

between the parts and the whole within the landscaped composition must exist in order for the viewer to feel comfortable within the space.

Second, because scale is relative to perception, it can be manipulated psychologically within the space. Manipulation of scale can be accomplished by utilizing certain tools. The following methods may be used to alter scale:

1. The size of the total space will offer certain limitations or advantages. Space in this connotation is relative to the lines of sight. Our ability to visualize is ordinarily unlimited except by physical barriers. Interior spaces are closed, with limiting boundaries; thus the ability to sculpture that space is limited. In the landscape design, however, the boundaries are virtually unlimited. The limits fall into two basic categories: *primary,* which are immediate limitations such as the ground, architectural structures, and on-site foliage; and *secondary,* which are limitations such as distant mountains, the sky, or foliage located off the site. These limitations serve as the basis for introducing scale in the design. If the area to be designed is open and relatively free of scenic barriers, the designer is left with many alternatives. On the other hand, a site that is confined visually by topography, neighboring structures, or existing foliage must be carefully analyzed to ensure adequate planning.
2. The designer can cause certain planes or surfaces within a space to appear either close or far in relation to the viewer through the selection of textures. A fine texture appears more distant than a coarse texture. Texture is created by several variations: size of units within a space; number of units within a space; and space between units (figure 3-19).
3. Color has an effect on our perception of scale. Darker

colors seem to recede and to be more distant, while lighter colors appear to be near. The human eye is unable to focus on adjacent colors when those colors lie opposite on the color wheel. For example, a mass of red flowers placed within a predominantly green environment has minimal effect unless there is another color that can be planted between them.

SEQUENCE

Sequence is characterized by continuity and connection from one element to another. It is imperative to any art form, especially a planting composition. The proper sequence of color or texture will allow a viewer's eye to move along or within the space in an orderly fashion.

Using color or texture in a rhythmic pattern adds harmony to the arrangement of plant materials. A fine-textured tree, shrub, or groundcover should blend into a medium-textured plant, which in turn should blend into a coarse texture—or the reverse. This is not to say that all three textures must be represented in every arrangement. Fine or coarse textures may need to flow only into medium textures to be effective in a composition; but fine textures should never blend into coarse textures without the buffer of a medium pattern present to maintain the transitional illusion.

Color supports design harmony when there is a blending of colors from dark to medium to light, or light to medium to dark. With color, a designer can support the textural sequence with a harmonious color sequence.

Spacing, which is relative to a plant's ultimate growing capacity, should also have transitional order. Undefined spacing patterns cause dramatic breaks in the visual harmony of a planting arrangement. To achieve sequence with spacing, a

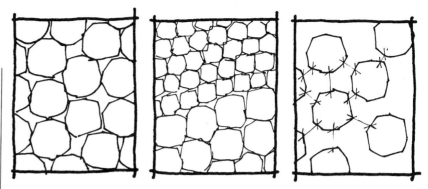

Figure 3-19. The size and number of units and the space between them will vary the perceived space.

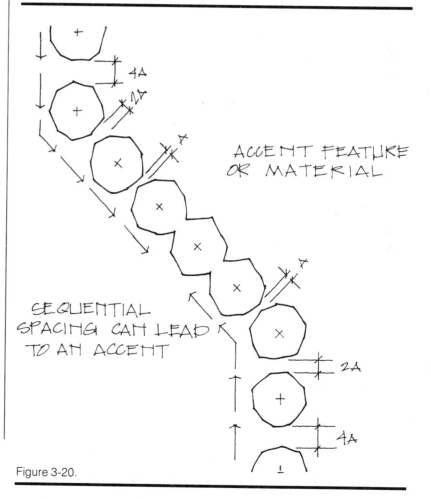

ACCENT FEATURE OR MATERIAL

SEQUENTIAL SPACING CAN LEAD TO AN ACCENT

Figure 3-20.

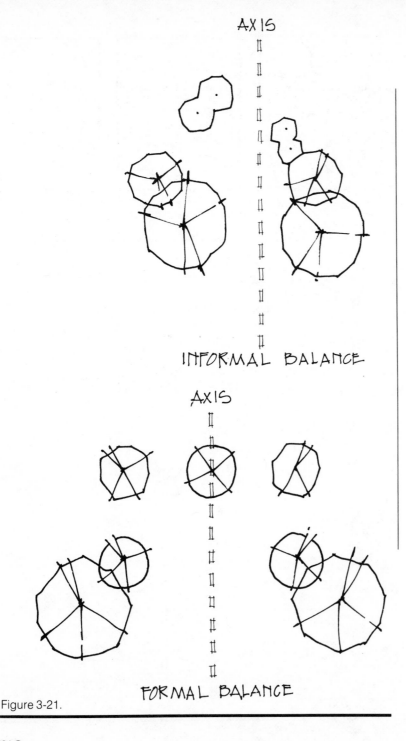

AXIS

INFORMAL BALANCE

AXIS

FORMAL BALANCE

Figure 3-21.

designer must pay attention to the spacing of a mass of plants as well as the spacing of individual materials (figure 3-20).

BALANCE

Balance is the state of equipoise between landscape-design elements. It is the "visual sense" you have as a planting designer, how you use masses, colors, lines, and textures, and how they appear to the viewer (figure 3-21).

In planting design, we consider two basic types of balance: *formal* or symmetrical, which is the repetition of features on each side of the central axis, often called mirror-image design; and *informal* or asymmetrical, the variation of plant type, quantity, or position on either side of the central axis.

Planting-design elements comprise the major ingredients of any landscape composition. The physical plant properties of color, form, and texture are applied to create specific accent, scale, sequence, or balance in an outdoor setting. Although these have been presented separately, they are not separate considerations.

The planting designer must go on to implement those techniques that allow for the final creation of the molded and shaped exterior space. To stop after considering only the first elements would present an environment that was merely decorated with plants.

4/IMPLEMENTATION

THE ARCHITECTURAL FORMS

As a plant occupies space, it may appear in either a primary or secondary architectural design form. The *primary* forms are the walls, the ceilings, or the floors. The *secondary* forms are the screens, the canopies, the barriers, the baffles, and the groundcovers (figures 4-1, 4-2).

The primary "wall" form is comprised of the screen, the barrier, and the baffle. The "ceiling" form is reinforced by the canopy, and the "floor" form is supported by the groundcover.

A "wall" functions as a shield against outside influences. It obstructs objectionable views, creates privacy, and protects the individual within a space (figure 4-3). A "ceiling" occupies the overhead space, and gives us shade, shelter, and protection from above (figure 4-4). A "floor" is the form that connects the other primary features, providing continuity and transition to planting compositions (figure 4-5).

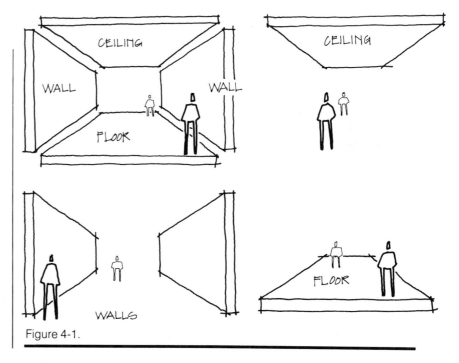

Figure 4-1.

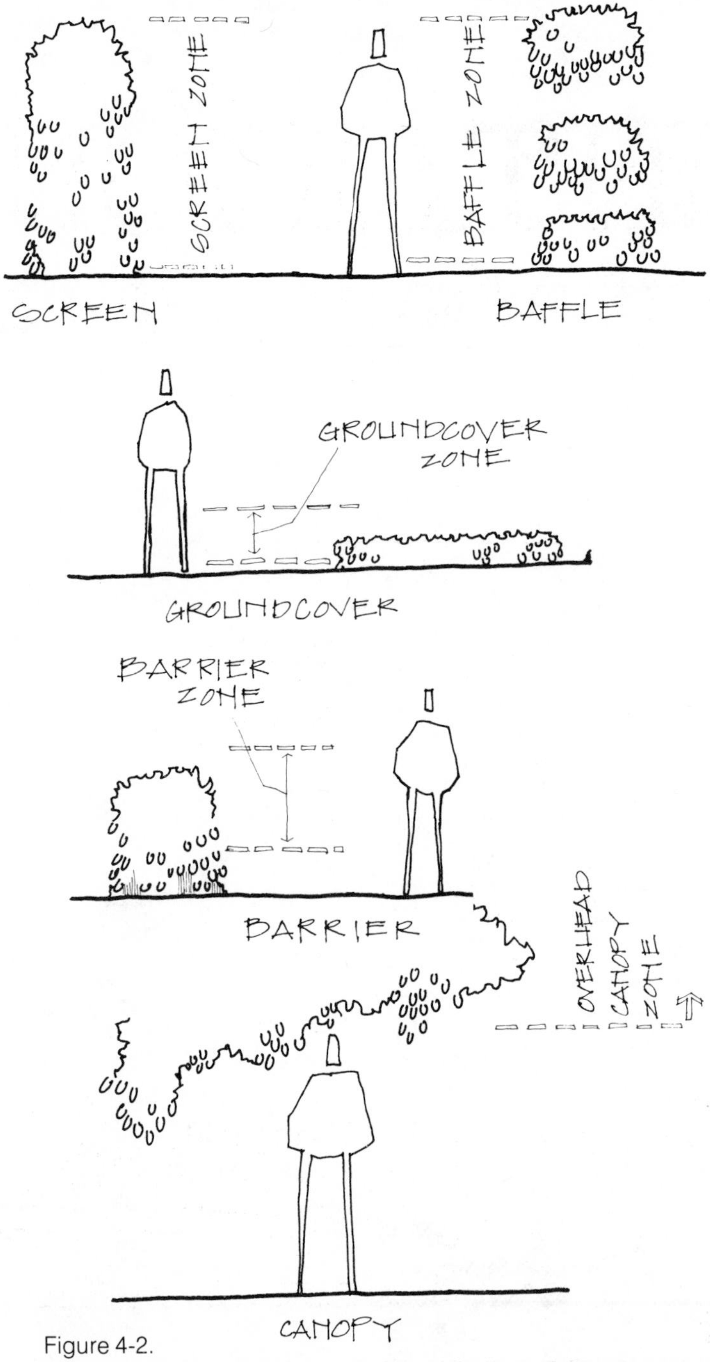

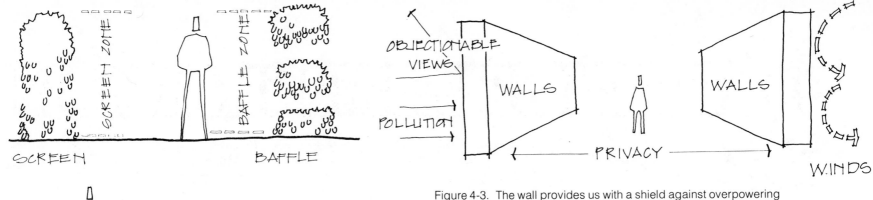

SCREEN   SCREEN ZONE   BAFFLE ZONE   BAFFLE

OBJECTIONABLE VIEWS

POLLUTION

WALLS

WALLS

PRIVACY

WINDS

Figure 4-3. The wall provides us with a shield against overpowering influences. It screens the objectionable views, provides privacy, and often protects us from the polluting materials in our environment.

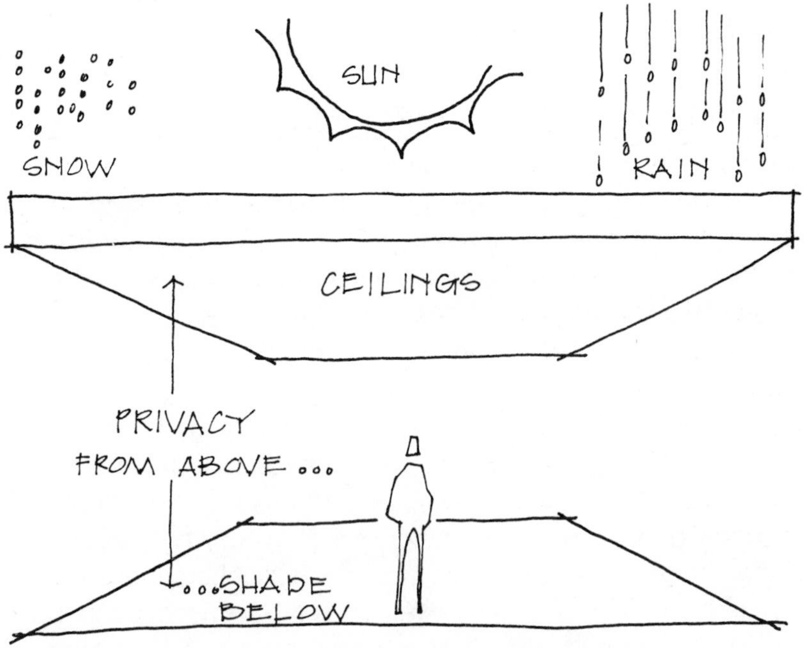

GROUNDCOVER ZONE

GROUNDCOVER

BARRIER ZONE

BARRIER

OVERHEAD CANOPY ZONE

CANOPY

Figure 4-2.

SNOW   SUN   RAIN

CEILINGS

PRIVACY FROM ABOVE...

...SHADE BELOW

Figure 4-4. The ceiling dominates our overhead space with either full or partial enclosure. It gives us shade on a hot summer afternoon, shelters us from nature's elements, and safeguards our environment from above.

A BERM AND SMALL SHRUB CAN BE USED AS A SCREEN...

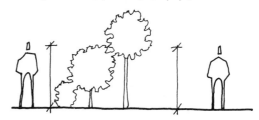

PLANT MASSES CAN CREATE A SCREEN....

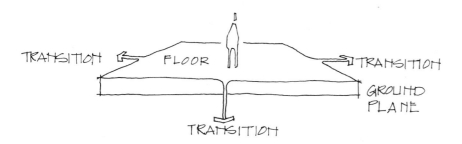

Figure 4-5. The floor is the ground plane of our outside environment. This design feature is the major element that connects one plant material type to another with flowing and continual transition.

The secondary architectural forms may be defined as follows:

1. The *screen* is a plant or plant mass used as a total enclosure of a landscape space. A person within the space cannot walk or see through this form. A screen may be created with a single plant, a plant mass, or a combination of plants with other landscape elements (figure 4-6).
2. The *canopy* is a plant or plant mass with a branching height of seven feet or more that will allow an individual to walk underneath. Its most important design characteristic is that it occupies only the overhead plane (figure 4-7). A canopy

SMALLER SHRUBS CAN BE COMBINED WITH STRUCTURES TO FUNCTION AS SCREENS...

Figure 4-7. Plants with drooping branches can create a canopy. The overhead plane is the important design factor.

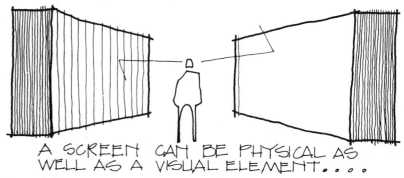

A SCREEN CAN BE PHYSICAL AS WELL AS A VISUAL ELEMENT....

Figure 4-6.

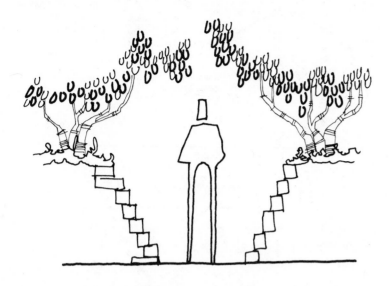

Figure 4-8. Small trees or large shrubs can create a canopy when combined with structural elements.

may be created by using a plant type that will occupy this spatial zone (figure 4-8).

3. The *barrier* is a plant or plant mass used as a partial enclosure or to control the circulation within a landscape space. A person may see over this feature but not pass through it (figure 4-9). A barrier may be created with a plant mass usually not below two feet or above five feet in height.

4. The *baffle* is a plant or plant mass that is used to control visual experiences within a landscape space. An individual within the space may see through but cannot walk through it. A baffle may be created by a plant or plant mass that does not interrupt the visual experience but does act as a physical barrier (figure 4-10).

5. The *groundcover* is a plant or plant mass used as a visual floor, usually reaching a maximum height of eighteen inches. It may be created by keeping the feature below the eye level of the individual within the space (figure 4-11).

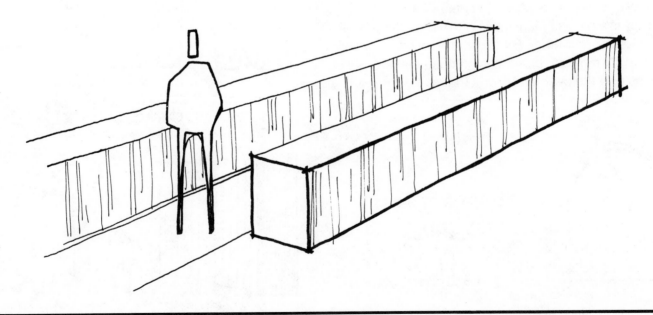

Figure 4-9.

These primary and secondary architectural forms may be used by the planting designer to create numerous and varied landscape compositions. The constraints for their effectiveness as a design feature, however, are as follows:

1. The type, age, and condition of the plant materials.
2. The spacing of the plants, which determines the opacity, translucency, or transparency of the element.
3. The form and growth rate of the individual plants, which affect the density of the total element. (Density is affected by the shape and size of the leaves, branching patterns, branching heights, and the height and width of the plant when planted and when mature.)

THE DESIGN COMPONENTS

As a designer considers the effects of a single plant or plant mass on the exterior environment, additional thought must be given to the way in which the viewer will react within the composition. The elements of color, form, texture, accent, scale, and sequence are the basic considerations in the application of various design components to a finished landscape. Combined with the architectural forms, the design components magnify the character of the molded space and allow the designer to control the way in which the space is both seen and felt by the viewer.

The *primary* design components are the physical units that support the design:

1. *Direction* moderates the physical movement within a landscape space. A designer may control the visual experiences within the composition by allowing movement only in a specific direction or area (figure 4-12).

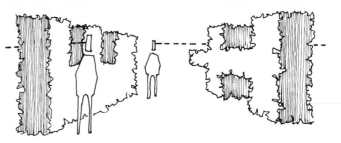

A LARGE PLANT MASS CAN CREATE A BAFFLE

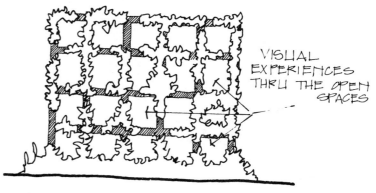

VISUAL EXPERIENCES THRU THE OPEN SPACES

A VINE ON A TRELLIS CAN CREATE A BAFFLE

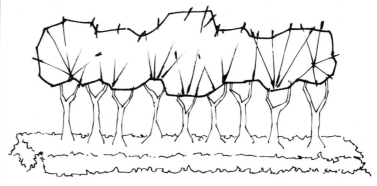

A GROUND COVER WITH SMALL TREES OR LARGE SHRUBS CAN CREATE A BAFFLE

Figure 4-10.

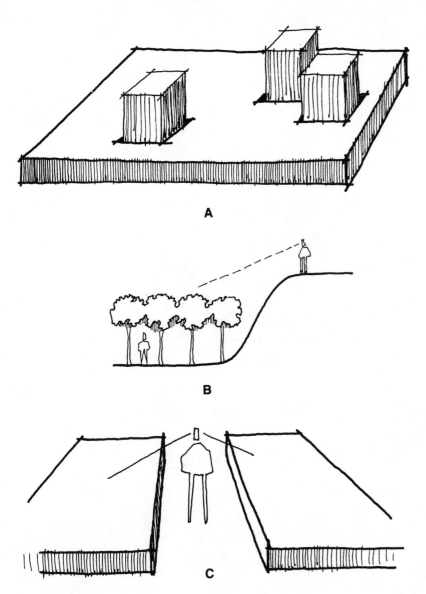

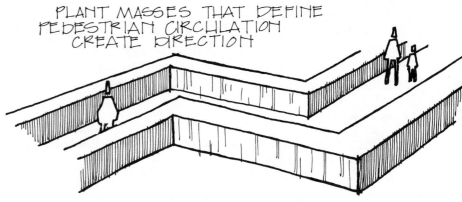

Figure 4-12.

Figure 4-11. (A) The groundcover is the major transition element in planting design; (B) a canopy can be a visual groundcover if seen from above; (C) the "below-eye-level plane" is the important design factor.

2. *Pooling*, on the other hand, defines the outdoor rooms desired by the designer. As viewers are directed throughout a composition, it may be desirable to expand the size of the perceived space and alter available experiences (figure 4-13).

The *secondary* components are the visual units that support the design:

1. *Enframement* draws attention to a focal area or important view within the composition or to an offsite feature. It may be accomplished by using trees or shrubs that project into the visual plane (figure 4-14).
2. *Linkage* visually joins one space or object to another space or object (figure 4-15).
3. *Enlargement* or *reduction* is the ability to change the apparent size of a composition. It may be accomplished by varying the degree of enclosure of the space.

A POOL IS CREATED WHEN THE PLANT MASSES DEFINE THE SPACE...

Figure 4-13.

4. *Invitation* denotes the use of stimulation, suggestion, or curiosity to pull a viewer into or through a space. It may be accomplished with moving objects or with bright, sudden changes of color (figure 4-16).
5. *Subdivision* is the use of plant materials to divide a large space into smaller components or to create a small space within a large one.

DEVELOPING A PRELIMINARY PLAN

As discussed in chapter 2, the actual development of the final concept for a planting environment begins in the preliminary phase of the design process. In developing the plan we use procedures that establish the design function of the materials—in effect, we use a process within a process.

Figure 4-14.

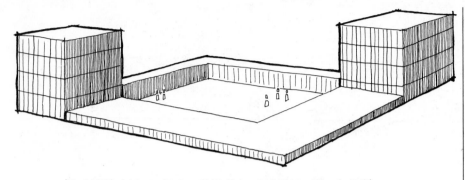

PLANT MASSES CAN BE USED TO LINK
ARCHITECTURAL ELEMENTS TOGETHER TO FORM
EXTERIOR POOLS

Figure 4-15.

This secondary operation expresses the general philosophy that the selection of a plant for a landscape composition should first be based upon its design function and then by its horticultural characteristics. Too often, landscapes exhibit the reverse, containing materials that are awkward for their location and creating the feeling of being "out of place."

Although both considerations are of critical importance to the total success of a composition, the approach of function before selection will allow a designer to adapt a design intent to almost any geographic region of the country.

The following procedures can be added to develop the design function of the plants and plant masses within a space:

1. *Determine the general design components of the composition.* With information obtained from the client's *design intent*, establish the primary design components by creating specific *pools* of space and a specific *direction* for pedestrian movement. Determine the necessary views that need to be *enframed* from various vantage points. Select which features should be *linked* together with plant masses and locate special materials that will *invite* the viewer's attention. If there is one large space, propose plant masses that will subdivide the composition into smaller areas (figure 4-17).
2. *Shape the space to achieve the primary architectural functions.* Use walls, ceilings, and floors to shape the composition. This is the beginning of the sculpturing process whereby the designer establishes control over the planting environment (figure 4-18).

Figure 4-16. Moving objects and sounds are excellent for creating invitation.The water fountain here, partially hidden by the use of berms, is inviting to the viewer. (Courtesy, Richard Myrick, Dallas, Texas)

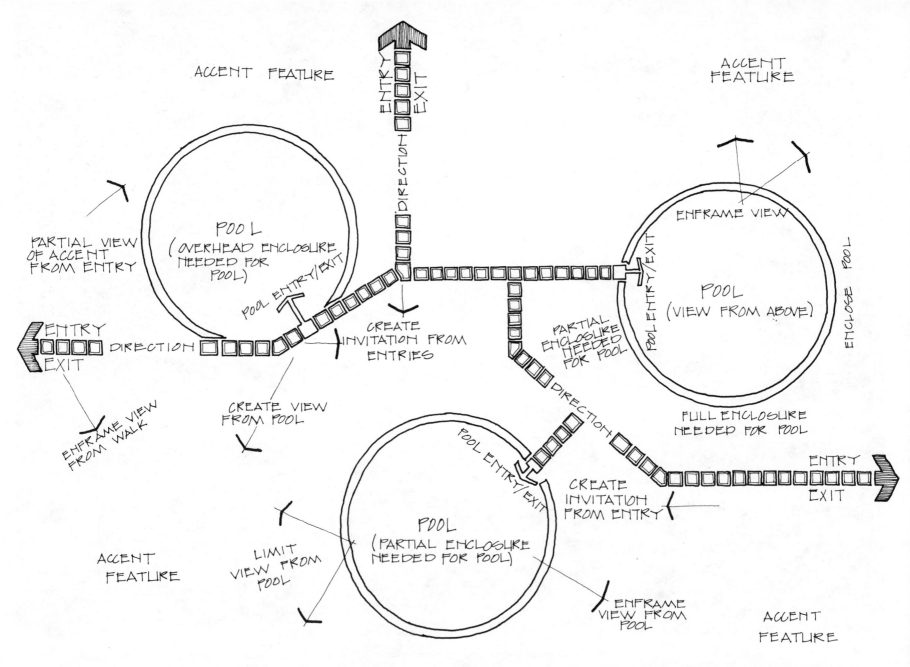

Figure 4-17. The general design components can be represented in basic schematic graphics. Identify the important features with bubble diagrams and then make notes on the important tasks to complete with the placement of plant materials.

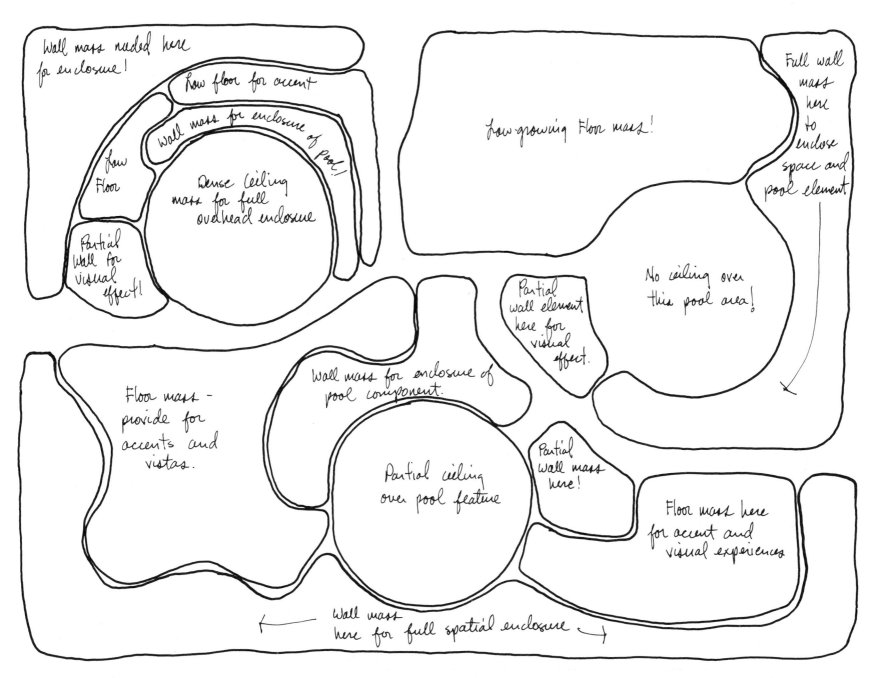

Figure 4-18. The shape of the outdoor space begins to emerge when *walls, ceilings,* and *floors* are selected to support the intent.

3. *Refine the space with the secondary architectural forms.* Establish the specific functions of each plant or plant mass by creating the spaces and effects needed in the *design intent*. Use the elements of *color*, *form*, *texture*, *accent*, *scale*, *sequence*, and *balance* to support the composition and provide specific means of selecting the plant materials needed in the design (figure 4-19).
4. *Select the design elements to reinforce the spatial objectives.* Develop a preliminary planting plan that meets the client's needs and allows full creative input from the designer (figure 4-20).

These extra steps should govern the plant selection for the given space. For example, it may now be determined that a dark green (foliage color), rounded (form), fine-textured, accent canopy is needed for a particular location within the composition.

Figure 4-19. (*Facing page*) The refinement of the composition begins with the placement of *screens, baffles, barriers, canopies,* or *groundcovers*. Once these are developed, the proper color, form and texture combinations can take place.

Mass A: dense screen to support the enclosure of the space from off-site elements

Mass B: low-height groundcover for viewing the accent feature

Mass C: medium-height groundcover as an accent element for the entry positions

Mass D: narrow screen to enclose and obstruct the accent feature from within the pool area

Mass E: baffle to allow the viewing of the accent feature from the pathway

Mass F: dense canopy for overhead enclosure

Mass G: low-growing groundcover for an "open" feeling

Mass H: small, bright accent shrub

Mass I: dense screen to enclose the space and pool area; helps divide the large space into smaller units

Mass J: baffle, for partial enclosure

Mass K: dense screen, for more complete enclosure of the pool feature

Mass L: low-growing groundcover

Mass M: dense screen for enclosure of the total space

Mass N: medium height accent shrub

Mass O: partial canopy for the pool feature.

Mass P: accent shrub for invitation

Mass Q: low-growing groundcover

Mass R: low, accent shrub

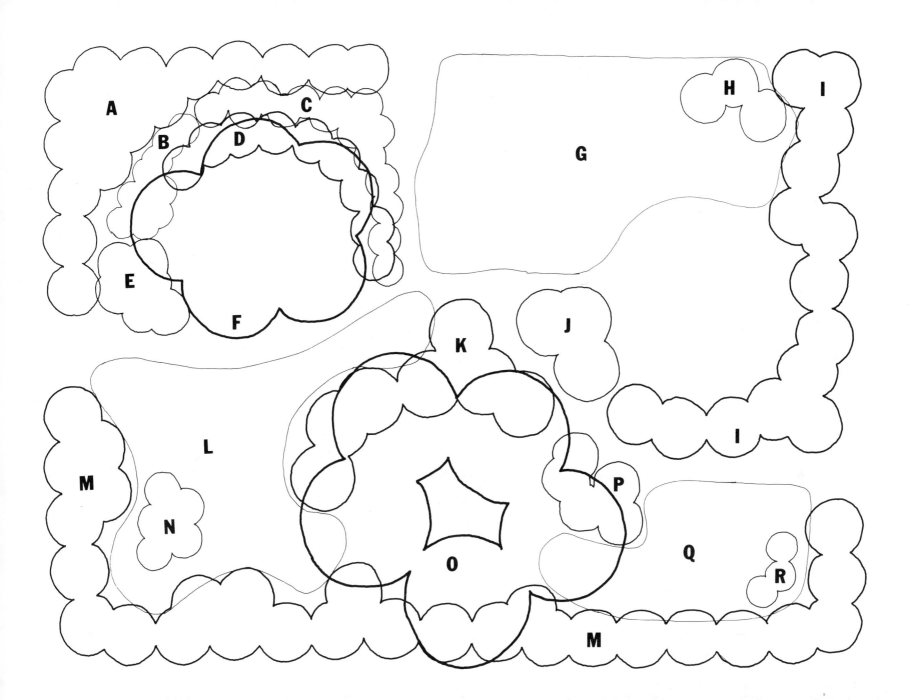

Figure 4-20. The finished planting plan represents the designer's objectives based upon the intent of the space. From this final plan, modifications (if required) will direct the construction of the composition.

PLANT APPLICATION

TREES

Trees are the most fundamental element in any planting environment. Because of their long life and high value, which increases with age, it is worth the time to give careful attention to their function, selection, and placement. Properly selected trees may be more permanent than most building structures; and, if care is taken during the planning process, they will add a great deal to the beauty and value of the space being developed.

One of the most important points to remember is that no single tree species can perform all the functions necessary for a successful landscape development. Trees should be planted to solve various problems and to fulfill several purposes. When selecting a tree, consider these uses:

1. *Shade.* Plant shade trees in the area where they will do the most good. The stronger-branched varieties may be planted closer to an architectural structure without fear of breakage. Fast-growing, weaker-branched trees should never be planted too near a structure because of possible damage during severe ice or windstorms.
2. *Enframement.* Some varieties of trees may also provide enframement (the framing of a view) for the approach to a structure. These plants should be placed just off the front corners or to the sides to give the lawn or architectural feature a specific accent.
3. *Screening.* Trees are useful for screening out undesirable views. When used in natural-growing clumps, they become

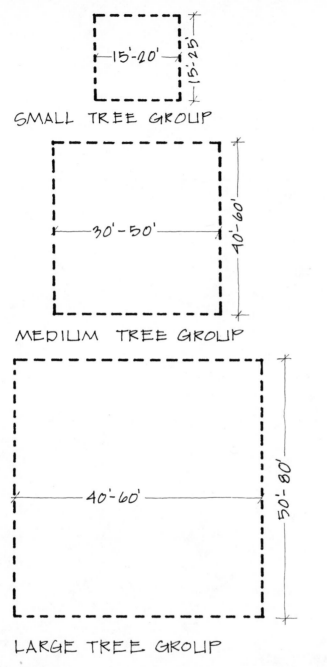

SMALL TREE GROUP

15'-20' 15'-25'

MEDIUM TREE GROUP

30'-50' 40'-60'

LARGE TREE GROUP

40'-60' 50'-80'

Figure 4-21.

objects of beauty in color or form and draw attention away from undesirable objects. They may also provide protection from summer or winter winds. Dense plantings of deciduous trees and perhaps some evergreen varieties are also effective barriers to harsh environmental elements.

4. *Growth rate and size*. Every tree variety has a characteristic growth rate. Slow-growing trees usually have less than eighteen inches of new growth each year. Medium-growing trees produce up to three feet of new shoots in a growing season. The fast-growing varieties, which produce more than three feet of growth a year, are most often planted in a residential landscape because they produce quick shade and add value more rapidly. However, do not make the mistake of planting only fast-growing varieties. Think of the environment's appearance in ten or fifteen years. The correct tree size to use in an environment is determined by the height and spread of the plant at maturity and the amount of space with which you have to work (figure 4-21). Small trees are generally thirty feet or less in height at maturity and work best in small gardens and miniature landscape settings. They include most of the ornamental flowering trees and many of the "patio" varieties. Medium trees most often attain a height between thirty and seventy feet at maturity and look well in the urban landscape setting. Medium trees do not become too tall for inner-city gardens or for landscapes around single-story homes. Large trees reach a mature height of seventy feet or more. They should be planted only in large spaces, such as extensive parks, where their branches will not intefere with each other. The width of a given tree varies with the individual species; this factor should be checked against its height before a specific selection is made.

SHRUBS

Shrubs provide many of the same design functions as trees—but at a different spatial scale. For all practical purposes, the shrub's particular application lies between the overhead canopy and the ground plane. A large shrub reaching a mature height as high as the overhead plane should be considered a small tree (figure 4-22). A small shrub growing horizontally along the ground should be used as a groundcover mass instead of as an individual plant. When selecting a shrub, consider these uses:

1. *Enframement.* A shrub can provide the framing component to special view into or away from a landscape space. However, due to its size, it may require support from a landform or construction feature. Place the shrub on either side of the intended accent and frame it as if it were a picture.

2. *Screening.* Large shrubs can screen undesirable views or provide a visual corridor into a landscape space. The object of the "screen" is to obstruct a view from one area into another. A small or medium shrub can also act as a screen if combined with a landform or construction feature.

3. *Accent.* Shrubs are very often used as accent features within a landscape space. As one of the most demanding functions, the species should be chosen and used with caution. Too many accents, or one that is too strong, will confuse the viewer and create disharmony within the composition.

GROUNDCOVERS

The term groundcover can be used to describe almost any plant in the landscape. It does, however, refer primarily to plant materials under eighteen inches in height, of spreading or

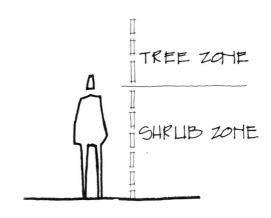

Figure 4-22.

creeping habit, that are used to hide unsightly areas of exposed ground.

The value of this plant feature can be easily measured in greatly reduced maintenance costs. With a mass of groundcover, less weeding will be required under trees and shrubs; severe erosion can be halted and controlled along steep banks; and the loss of water from soil due to sun exposure can be halted.

There are two functional classes of groundcovers. The first is the lawn substitute, used to cover a large expanse of ground and give the general appearance of a lawn. This use requires the same careful soil preparation, the same initial weeding requirements, and often the same winter hardiness as grass. Therefore, little, if any, energy conservation can be found by using this type of groundcover. The second class is the ornamental groundcover. These are used to decorate walks with borders, cover the ground where grass will not grow, and add beauty and accent to shrub masses.

A *vine* can be a groundcover growing on a mechanical structure. When combined with a trellis, decorative fence, or wire frame, this plant element can be used where space is limited or as a canopy, baffle, screen, or barrier.

Vines climb in very specific patterns, and each pattern should be understood before it is used in an environment. Vines climb in the following ways:

1. *Twining* is characterized by a vertical, twisting growth pattern as plants grasp small posts or other plants. Both vertical and top supports are needed. These types of vines tend to become top-heavy.
2. *Tendrils* are "fingers" that cling and fasten to a support.
3. *Clinging* is a habit of growth that allows that plant to adhere to flat surfaces.

4. *Weaving* is exhibited by a vine with younger, growing shoots that wrap through older branches.
5. *Leaning* is shown by a plant that may also be a shrub with climbing shoots that may grow against a structure or a tree trunk.

ELEMENT APPLICATIONS

When using any tree, shrub, groundcover, or vine, it is important to remember these elements of design.

FLOWER AND FOLIAGE COLORS

Flowering materials add interest to any planting design and care should be taken in their selection. Use flowering plants together to extend the blooming season and to maintain the visual appearance of the total composition.

Foliage color is often considered when selecting a tree or a shrub. However, some groundcover and vine species are brilliant in the spring and fall and should not be overlooked. (Do not expect all plants to produce bright red or gold colorations every autumn. The pigments that produce the hues and tints are dependent upon proper light and temperature combinations during the early autumn months.)

FORM

The shape of a plant at maturity is an important consideration before selection is made. The round or broadly spreading forms of trees provide the best shade. Shrubs with this shape also produce a more dramatic effect when allowed to grow without competition from other plants.

Oval-shaped trees appear best in groups if the desired effect is shade because they produce a less abundant sunscreen than do the round forms. Pyramidal plants provide poor shade because they are narrowest at the top and cast a pointed shadow with only a small amount of shade. Columnar plants can provide a screen or be used in a narrow planting space. They often soften the lines of a building or home. Weeping or drooping forms provide dramatic accents in a design space and can act as a visual link between an overhead canopy and a ground plane.

LOCATION CONSIDERATIONS

Proper planning of each location will allow many years of trouble-free maintenance. Here are some locations that should be avoided whenever possible:

1. Do not plant trees closer than four to five feet from drives or walks. As they grow to maturity, the root system may cause cracks and separations in the paving elements.
2. Do not plant trees or large shrubs under overhead wires. Utility companies have the right to prune the branches without the owner's permission (in most cases) and the results may not meet your design objectives.
3. Do not plant weak, fast-growing trees closer than thirty to forty feet from a structure. These trees are easily damaged by winds and ice storms, and the branches may fall and cause damage.
4. Do not overplant. A few good specimens in a mass arrangement are better than a large number of overcrowded, single-species arrangements.
5. Do not plant trees or large shrubs closer than one to one and one-half times their spread from sewer, water, or septic lines.
6. Do not plant trees or large shrubs too close to windows or doors or directly in front of a structure. If you do, you may hide attractive architectural characteristics.

PLANTING SUGGESTIONS

The planting techniques chosen determine the success or failure of the materials used in a design. A plant will not reach its full potential if placed incorrectly in the composition. Follow these general rules in order to reach the optimum growing conditions:

1. Select a location where a plant has enough room to reach maturity. Crowding plants may cause excessive competition for light, soil nutrients, and growing space. When planting, use the measurements of the mature spread of plants to determine location.
2. Choose the time of planting carefully. Some deciduous trees are best planted while dormant. Most evergreen materials can be planted during any season as long as care is taken to maintain a soil ball around the root system.
3. Excavate a generous planting pit and add soil amendments as required by the geographic area. If the soil is too heavy or too sandy, it will benefit from a healthy addition of organic matter such as peat or humus.
4. Plant as soon as the material is purchased from the nursery or collected from the field. Waiting too long may increase the "shock" a plant encounters when being moved.
5. Trees more than four inches in caliper (diameter) should be supported with guy wires. This allows the growing position to be corrected as the soil around the root system settles.

ENVIRONMENTAL INSULATION

One form of insulation that has been overlooked by many designers is that provided by plant materials. The plants that you choose for your environment can serve not only aesthetic

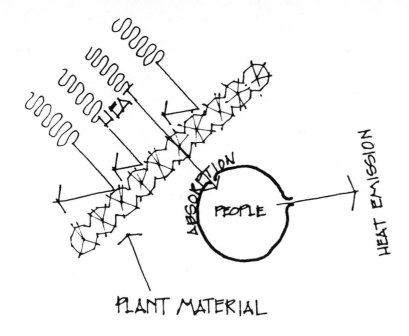

PLANT MATERIAL

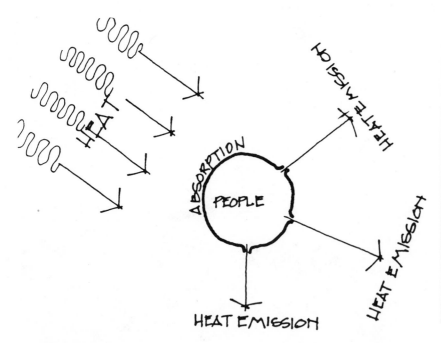

Figure 4-23.

and food-supplement purposes but also that of energy conservation.

Insulation is now recognized as the essential link in the chain of comprehensive energy conservation, and the unique character of the insulation becomes the most important factor in the establishment of a desirable living environment.

As humans, we receive and emit heat. We absorb it either from a direct temperature source, or from a reflected source, or by conduction (the transmission of heat from particle to particle). We radiate heat in much the same fashion. Our comfort is reached when there is a balance of heat emission and heat absorption (figure 4-23).

Landscape plant materials act as a supplementary insulation resource supporting the attainment and maintenance of our comfort requirements. Plants can be the first line of defense to absorb, reflect, or filter the extreme temperature elements, allowing cellulose, asbestos, or synthetic materials to perform at their highest efficiency.

The heat we receive in our day-to-day living begins some ninety million miles away on the surface of the sun. As this solar radiation begins its journey to the surface of the earth, it comes into contact with high-level clouds, causing some of it to be reflected back into the atmosphere. Other rays strike small air particles and become diffused, while even more rays are absorbed by carbon dioxide and water vapor. The remaining radiation, approximately one-fifth of the initial amount, reaches us and affects the way we live.

Landscape plant materials are the best first-line exterior barriers for insulating solar radiation. We have only to look at the natural organization of landscape plants to support this claim. In tropical climates, where the sun becomes continually oppressive, large and thick plants that provide shade to animals unadapted to living in the extreme heat predominate. In the colder climates, plants shed their leaves in order to allow increased radiation to reach the earth's surface during the colder periods.

Canopy elements can shade the roof surface of the environment, allowing for cooler air temperatures below. Shrubs and vines can diffuse and reflect solar radiation away from the space and allow for a cooler area for human use. The ground-plane element can assist in absorbing solar radiation and will prevent additional heat from being reflected into the landscaped environment.

With each change in season, large volumes of air begin to move around the surface of the earth at different velocities. As this air moves, winds of different intensities and temperatures are created, which bring to us pleasant cooling breezes or undesirable, often violent, windstorms. Most of the scientific knowledge regarding plants and wind control was obtained during the 1930s from the shelterbelt programs established throughout the Great Plains. It is from this program that we have learned to use plants to help control living environments.

Landscape plant materials can assist the designer in controlling wind by obstructing its flow, guiding it in a specific direction, deflecting its direction, and filtering its momentum. Obstructing wind with large shrubs and trees reduces its speed and thus reduces the strain on other more conventional forms of insulation. If plants are combined with landforms or architectural elements, you can create a very pleasing climate-controlling feature (figure 4-24).

Carefully placed shrub rows and small trees can guide a slow breeze through a porch, patio, or outdoor room. A solid mass of dense plantings can deflect a strong winter wind away from a large glass door, reducing its exposure to the cold. An

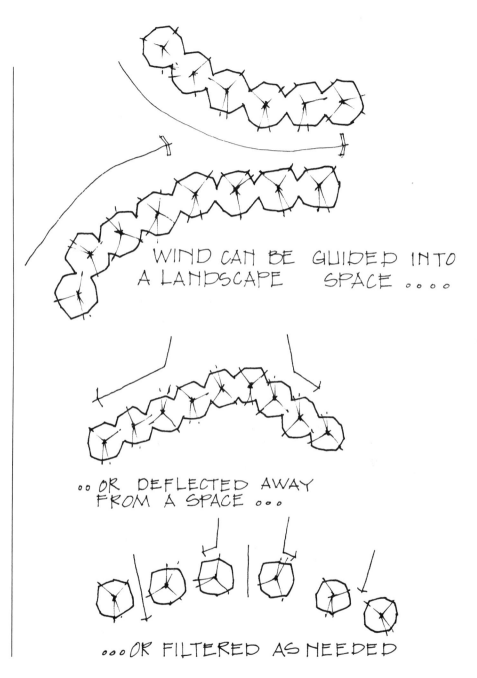

WIND CAN BE GUIDED INTO A LANDSCAPE SPACE ....

.. OR DEFLECTED AWAY FROM A SPACE ...

... OR FILTERED AS NEEDED

Figure 4-24.

open spacing of trees and shrubs can filter a strong wind, allowing a reduced-velocity breeze to reach a specific area for added comfort.

Selecting the proper plant type is very important in controlling wind. Deciduous trees and shrubs are good for filtering cold winds in the winter but are relatively ineffective for obstructing, guiding, or deflecting. Evergreen trees, while useful in the cold winter, may block the more desirable air movements in the spring and summer months.

Every designer understands that trees often protect individuals from rainfalls during a light or medium spring shower. As a matter of fact, plant canopies can eliminate from 60 to 80% of the falling water that may reach the environment below. The structure of the canopy, however, is the main controlling element—not the size of the tree. The amount of water that eventually reaches the ground is influenced by the intensity and duration of the rain, the use of an evergreen or deciduous tree, and the structure of the tree canopy.

The leaf arrangement and condition affects the canopy's structure. Evergreen or softwood trees have a leaf pattern that creates a greater number of sharp angles, which tend to trap water droplets. Large-leafed deciduous trees often only deflect the rain away from its original direction.

It is important to remember to select the tree for its structure and not its size if you want to inhibit the rainfall reaching the surface area of your design. Landscape plants can control sleet and snow by intercepting the crystals and directing the wind to alter the location of drifts.

Sleet and snow are usually held on the surfaces of leaves, branches, or needles because of the lower velocity of the flakes. This factor allows the designer more control of this cold element in the design. As wind velocity is slowed, ice particles are deposited near the plant and not toward other features of the space.

STREET PLANTINGS

A major factor in the environmental improvement of urban neighborhoods and rural communities is the establishment of a landscape development program. Too often, however, the orientation is toward the planting only of "street trees" and not to the overall character of the planting environment.

The landscape designer needs to look beyond the use of tree canopies and consider the total relationship of the spaces to be developed. The first step in any planting program is to inventory the neighborhood or community and identify the existing conditions of the project areas. Categories should be developed to relate to the degree of existing vegetation:

1. *Unwooded street*: vegetation exists on less than 30% of the project area.
2. *Semi-wooded street:* vegetation exists on more than 60%, but less than 80%, of the project area.
3. *Wooded street*: vegetation exists on more than 80% of the project area.

From the inventory, functional categories (based on growth habits) can then be applied to project needs (figure 4-25):

1. *Overhead zone materials* are the major covering components; they have large, dense crowns of foliage and are used to provide greater visual impact into and within the project area.
2. *Intermediate zone materials* are eye-level plantings of screens and baffles that are used to define the spaces on either side of the street core. As an understory feature, they can also be used to accent large architectural site elements and to serve as specimen plantings for environmental controls.

95

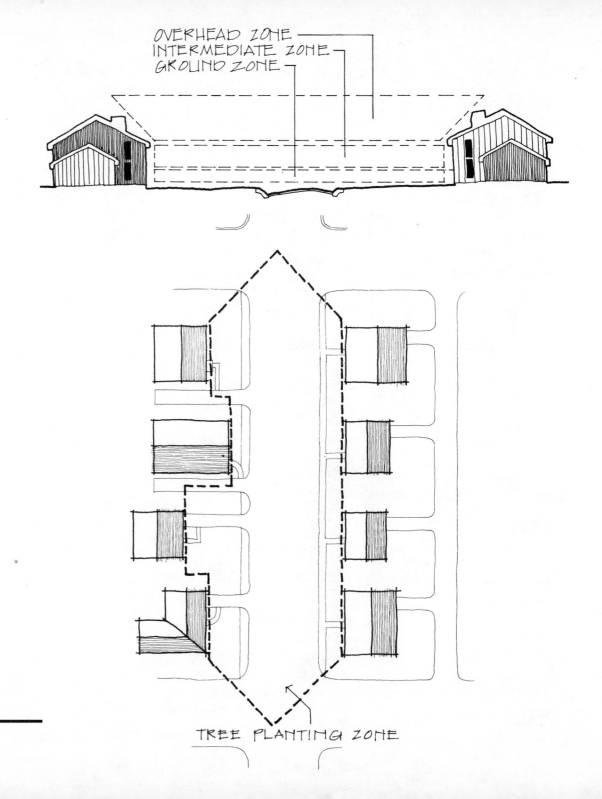

OVERHEAD ZONE
INTERMEDIATE ZONE
GROUND ZONE

TREE PLANTING ZONE

Figure 4-25.

3. *Ground zone materials* are small shrubs and groundcovers used to accent the ground spaces and to identify and control pedestrian areas within the development.

WILDLIFE HABITATS

Animals, like people, seek a landscaped environment for very special reasons. People often search for the solitude of space to rest from the complications of the day. Animals, on the other hand, need from the space the three essentials for their survival: food, shelter, and protection from predators.

Birds and small mammals are the easiest to attract because ornamental plant materials can be used for food, shelter, and protection. Food (and water) is found in the form of seeds, nuts, fruits, berries, and nectar or even the insects that are attracted to these. Shelter from the elements and protection from predators can be an individual plant, a plant mass, or a landform created to support a design.

General habitat design should follow a more natural approach if you wish the animals to stay in the space for any length of time. Rotten trees or stumps can be left or added to enhance the overall character of the composition. Remember, however, to relate the carrying capacity of the site to the needs of the wildlife. Too many animals are a negative factor and upset the capability of the designed environment to support the birds or small mammals you may need for your design intent.

SUPPORTING THE PLANTS IN YOUR DESIGN

The lack of availability of landscape plants often plays a negative role in some program developments. A scarcity of ornamental varieties that is caused by diseases or supply shortages makes some creative concepts unattractive or even impossible. To fill this void, the planting designer often uses several alternative materials to take the place of plants.

STONE

The most popular of these material is stone. Appearing as either layered outcroppings or large accent boulders, this feature can add interesting characteristics to a planting environment. The aesthetic qualities of stone are often quite striking, but its functional aspect is the key to successful application. Flat, rounded, or layered stones provide cool soil temperatures for the plants that need this habitat in order to survive. For this reason, all plants do not function with all stones. Some important factors when using stone are:

1. Allow soil pockets to collect below and between the stones. This provides the shade needed to support plant growth.
2. Do not place stones perpendicular to the soil base. This does not allow the stones to protect the soil for plant growth.
3. Allow only a portion of a large stone to appear above ground; expose only the weathered part.
4. If stratified material is used, make sure that all stones follow the same formation.
5. With a large collection of stone material, use large boulders for the central elements and support them with smaller ones around the edges of the composition.

WATER

Another popular alternative material is water. As a reflecting pool, a producer of soothing sounds, or a supplier of moisture for exotic plants, water can be an excellent support element for planting designs. It can be represented in large ponds, small pools, streams, or creeks and can be easily controlled for quality and quantity. A small pool or fountain can provide color or texture elements to support a transitional flow into an accent feature. When combined with lights or moving objects, water can be an important design feature for any planting composition.

Plants and water work well together in a design composition. Some plant varieties need only to be placed near water, while others—the aquatic plants—can be planted in water. Aquatic varieties can be classified as deep aquatics, marginal aquatics, or floating aquatics and can be used in an environment in the following manner (figure 4-26):

1. *Deep aquatics* require a depth of usually more than ten inches to survive. The roots of these plants can be planted in the base soil or in containers resting on the bottom of the water feature. These plants are important for the production of oxygen in the water.
2. *Marginal aquatics* grow with their roots in shallow water and have their crowns (stems, leaves, and flowers) above the waterline. They do not produce any measurable amounts of oxygen for the water.
3. *Floating aquatics* float on the surface with their roots exposed and not in any soil base. They reduce the amount of sunlight reaching the water below, thus reducing the amount of algae.

SCREENS AND FENCES

In an area where functional space is critical, a landscape designer may choose a decorative screen or fence to support a planting composition. A screen is merely a freestanding visual barrier, while a fence functions more as a physical barrier.

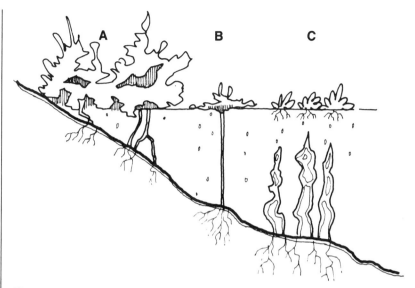

Figure 4-26. (*A*) Marginal aquatics; (*B*) floating aquatics; and (*C*) deep aquatics.

Construction materials for either feature can vary from wood to glass to brick; the choice for a given planting design should be determined by the available space. Screens or fences can be used independently from plants, in association with small shrubs or groundcovers, or as the framework for the support of vines or climbing groundcovers.

BERMS

On the other hand, when space is relatively open and lacking in aesthetic character, the designer may choose to use modified landforms—or berms—to enhance the plantings. Berms are mounds of soil, used when visual niches or vistas are needed in the composition. This feature should not dominate the space but work with the plant materials to support the overall intent (figure 4-27).

PLANT CONTAINERS

If growing areas are lacking or the environmental control needed by the selected plants is limited, containers are a popular alternative to conventional planting techniques. Useful for the introduction of annuals or exotic species into a composition, the container itself should not be the major concern of the planting designer. The plants in the container are still the most important considerations, and regular design approaches should be used in solving design problems with these plants. This does not mean, however, that attractive containers should be avoided. Brick, clay, and decorative pots always add an attractive theme to any landscape setting.

DESIGNING THE NATURAL LANDSCAPE

The one issue in planting design that almost always sparks debate and controversy is the subject of the natural landscape

Figure 4-27. The planting berm should work with and blend into the landscape composition.

composition. What it is, how it works, and how it is to be represented are sometimes lost in the arguments over the definitions of "natural" and "native" landscapes.

To solve this problem, the planting designers need only look at the relationships between the two terms. A *natural* landscape is based upon features that occur and exist within nature. A *native* landscape belongs to or originates in a particular place. "Natural" plants have been placed within a specific geographic region by the processes of nature. "Native" plants may originally be from one area but, due to human manipulation, are able to grow and thrive in another.

Since the majority of the ornamental plants we use in a design fall within the category of "native," the design compositions we create are technically not natural. A natural composition should consist of only plant materials found in the immediate geographic region. If an alternate native material is used, the final composition will fall within the ornamental classification.

The following principles may help in developing a natural landscape setting:

1. The final composition should lack formality and repetition of elements. The plants should be placed according to their environmental needs first—and then according to their design functions. No artificial or mechanical devices should be used to supplement growing conditions.
2. The design forms should follow the basic life forms (see chapter 1) as they are found naturally.
3. The composition should represent, as closely as possible, the successional stage in which the plant materials are found.
4. If plants die, they should not be removed. They should be allowed to decompose according to natural conditions.

5/GRAPHICS

THE NEED FOR THE PLANTING PLAN

The planting plan serves as the basic communication tool for the implementation of the planting design and is the primary link between the client, the designer, and the contractor.

The client needs the plan to obtain a clear understanding of the activities that will take place on the site. The planting plan also serves as an instrument for establishing a development budget for the client and the contractor.

The landscape contractor needs the plan to install the plant materials according to the designer's specifications. The plan that is used by the contractor becomes a sheet of specifications for construction and implementation. For this purpose, it should include formal planting specifications and construction and planting details. All information necessary to implement the plan in a satisfactory manner should be placed on the plan, and one should not depend on any verbal explanations to the contractor. The landscape contractor also uses a planting plan as a basis for price setting, labor determinations, tool requirements, and the acquisition of plant materials.

Planting plans may also be used to contract for plant materials from nurseries in advance of need and construction. Since many unique and rare plant types are becoming more difficult to find, this use should be of primary importance.

For the landscape designer, the plan serves as an instrument of communication in the creation or modification of the landscaped environment. It is with the planting plan that the designer creates the environment best suited to the client and, with the assistance of the landscape contractor, implements the design program on behalf of the client.

THE COMPONENTS OF THE PLANTING PLAN

The sheet layout for the planting plans is also important and should be well composed. The plan contains a tremendous amount of information, and the arrangement of all the plan components should be taken into careful consideration. The following outline contains the necessary components to be located on the plan. It should be noted, however, that this list will vary according to the size of the project and the scale of the drawing. For example, in order to obtain a manageable scale on large projects, more than one drawing may be necessary. However, only one plant schedule should be necessary for each project.

A. Scale, both written and graphic
B. North arrow
C. Existing plant materials
D. Plants to be removed or relocated

E. Structures, overhangs, paving (both existing and proposed)
F. Topography where applicable
G. Details where needed (a separate sheet is usually required)
H. Small orientation map
I. Title block
  1. Name of project
  2. Address of project
  3. Landscape architect
    a. Name
    b. Address of firm
    c. Registration seal
  4. Name or initials of drafter
  5. Date
  6. Page number
J. Plan schedule
  1. Item number (or symbol if used)
  2. Number of plants
    a. On location
    b. Totals
  3. Plant name
    a. Common name
    b. Botanical name
    c. Variety name
  4. Size and condition of plant
    a. Size
      (1) Container
      (2) Height of plant
      (3) Caliper
    b. Condition
      (1) Size of container
      (2) Balled and burlapped (B&B)
      (3) Bare root (B.R.)

5. Spacing for shrubs and groundcovers
6. Notes when required, such as "multitrunk" or "es-paliered"
7. Plant divisions (by trees, shrubs, and groundcovers)
8. Cost estimate (or space for contractor/bidder to supply cost figures)

K. Turf areas (on both plan and plant schedule; if turf is existing, it should appear only on the plan as existing)

BASIC GRAPHIC TECHNIQUES

The planting plan is essentially a construction document. It communicates specific planting requirements for the materials chosen for a landscaped environment. With this in mind, the planting designer should prepare the final plan to direct the installation of the materials—possibly by someone other than a member of the design team.

The following graphic techniques are the most commonly used for the preparation of a planting plan:

I. Symbolic (figure 5-1)
  A. Characteristics
    1. Plants are keyed
    2. Key is linked to a symbol on the plant key
    3. Symbols are placed upon a general site plan with no rendering
  B. Advantages
    1. Easy to place on drawing
    2. Gives accurate location of plants
    3. Used primarily by general contractors and engineers
    4. Can be used in highly complicated plans
    5. Takes very little time to produce

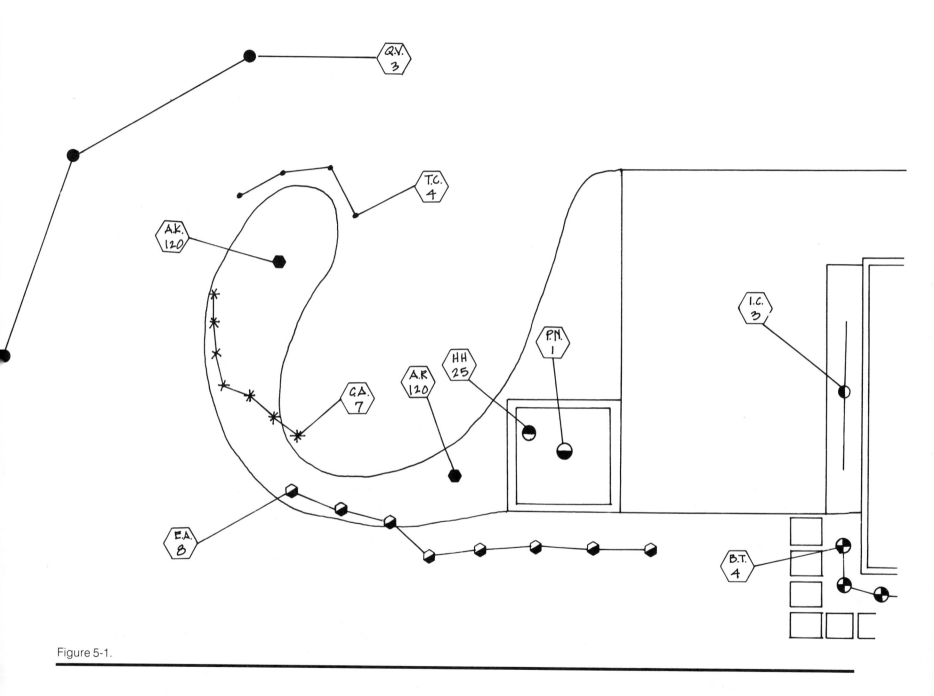

Figure 5-1.

C. Disadvantages
1. Does not represent plant masses
2. Does not give the client a clear example of actual plantings
3. Difficult to find symbols for all plants (for example, four sizes of one plant type)
4. Does not represent plant size on sheet

II. Semi-symbolic (figure 5-2)
A. Characteristics
1. Shows size relationship for plants
2. Plants are keyed
3. Key is linked to a plant list
4. No rendering
B. Advantages
1. Easy to place on drawings
2. Gives exact location of plants
3. Used primarily by landscape contractors
4. More easily understood by client
5. Takes very little time to produce
C. Disadvantages
1. Inconvenient to link symbols to plant list
2. Difficult to find symbols for all plants
3. Finished product is not always clear

III. Symbolic Representational (figure 5-3)
A. Characteristics
1. Plants have representational form
2. Rendering is common
3. Name of plant is used
4. Plants are not keyed
B. Advantages
1. Plants' forms and shapes are more easily understood by client

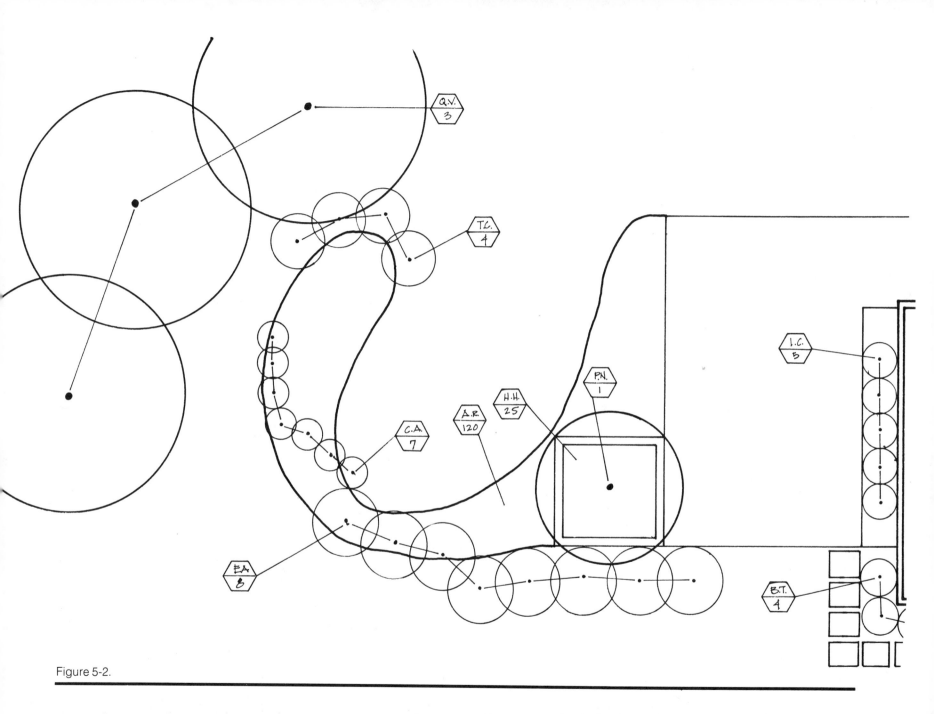

Figure 5-2.

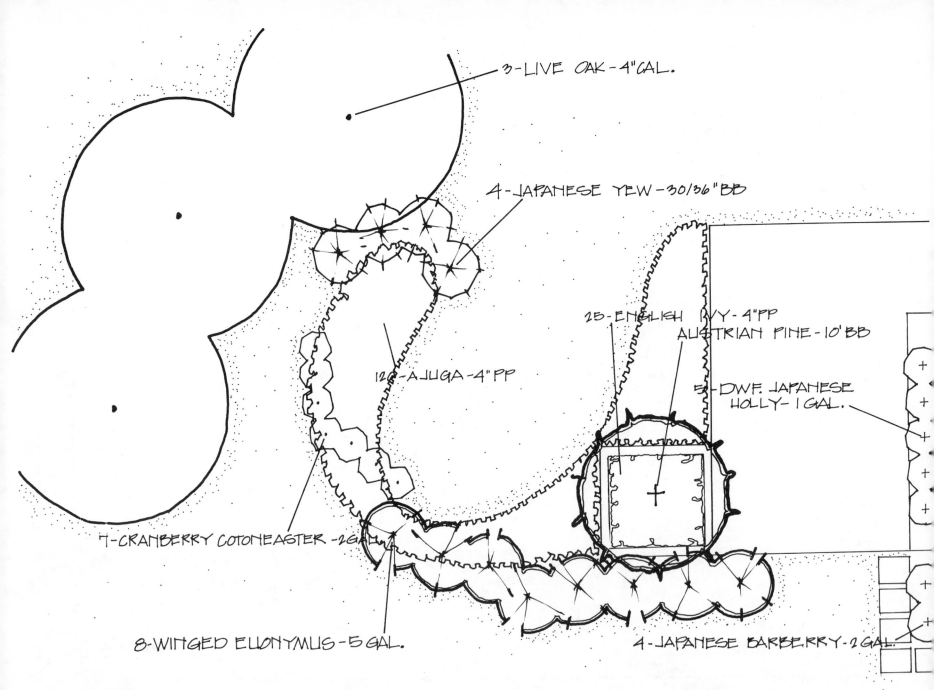

3-LIVE OAK-4"GAL.

4-JAPANESE YEW-30/36"BB

25-ENGLISH IVY-4"PP
AUSTRIAN PINE-10'BB

120-AJUGA-4"PP

5-DWF. JAPANESE
HOLLY-1 GAL.

7-CRANBERRY COTONEASTER-2GAL.

8-WINGED EUONYMUS-5 GAL.

4-JAPANESE BARBERRY-2GAL.

Figure 5-3.

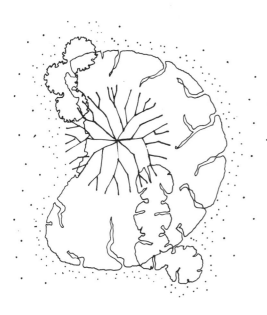

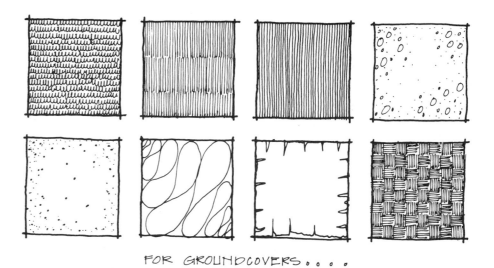

FOR GROUNDCOVERS....

OTHER TECHNIQUES FOR REPRESENTING
PLANT MASSES INCLUDE:

FOR TREE AND SHRUB MASSES....

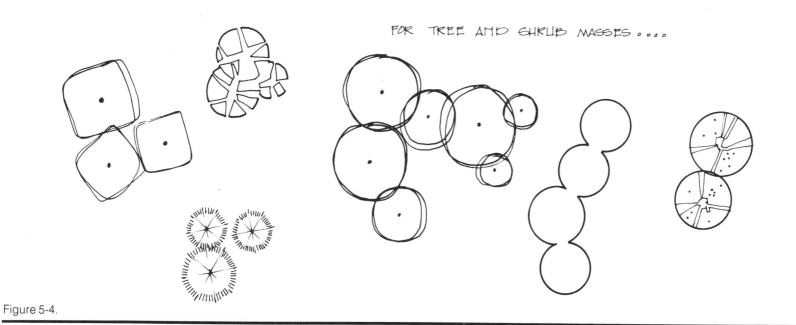

Figure 5-4.

2. Gives fairly accurate location of plants
3. Good for client presentations
4. Takes moderate amount of time for completion
C. Disadvantages
1. Plan can get too busy for complicated arrangements

To illustrate specific planting requirements, a designer may need concept sketches to support the communications effort. Examples of sketches used primarily to support the planting plan are shown in figures 5-5, 5-6, and 5-7. The planting plans shown in figures 5-8 through 5-15 have been contributed as representative samples of the landscape-design industry.

Figure 5-5. A quick pencil sketch will often illustrate your planting concepts to the client.

Figure 5-6. A more detailed line drawing can be used in formal presentations to client groups. (Courtesy, Larry Enersen, Lincoln, Nebraska)

Figure 5-7. A watercolor rendering can illustrate design concepts as well as final planting arrangements.

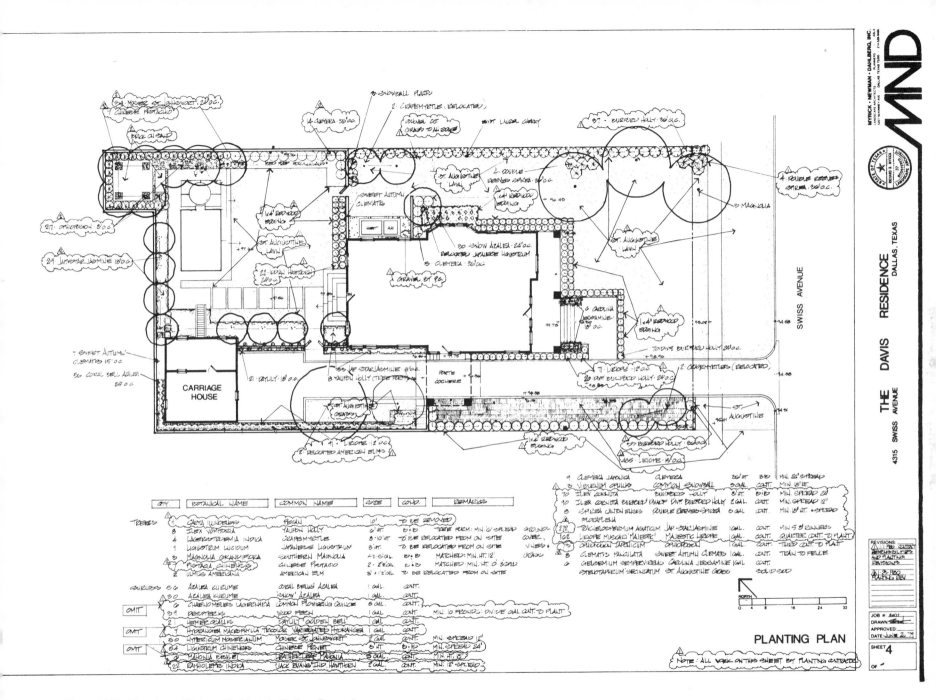

Figure 5-8. (Courtesy, Richard B. Myrick, Dallas, Texas.)

115

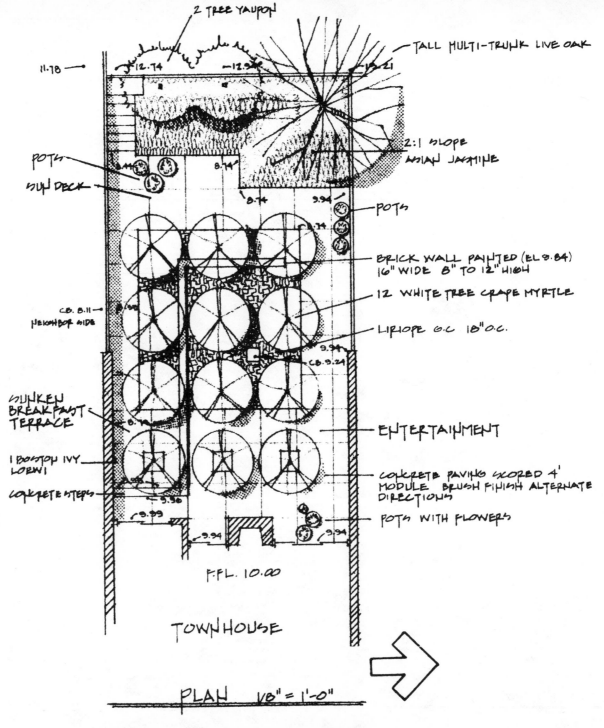

2 TREE YAUPON

TALL MULTI-TRUNK LIVE OAK

11.78

12.74

12.94

13.21

POTS

SUN DECK

8.14

9.94

2:1 SLOPE
ASIAN JASMINE

POTS

BRICK WALL PAINTED (EL 8.84)
16" WIDE 8" TO 12" HIGH

12 WHITE TREE CRAPE MYRTLE

C.B. 8.11
NEIGHBOR SIDE

LIRIOPE O.C. 18" O.C.

9.94

C.B. 9.24

SUNKEN
BREAKFAST
TERRACE

ENTERTAINMENT

1 BOSTON IVY
LOEWI

CONCRETE STEPS

9.50

CONCRETE PAVING SCORED 4'
MODULE BRUSH FINISH ALTERNATE
DIRECTIONS

POTS WITH FLOWERS

9.99

9.94

9.94

F.FL. 10.00

TOWNHOUSE

PLAN   1/8" = 1'-0"

116

Figure 5-9. (Courtesy, Richard B. Myrick, Dallas, Texas.)

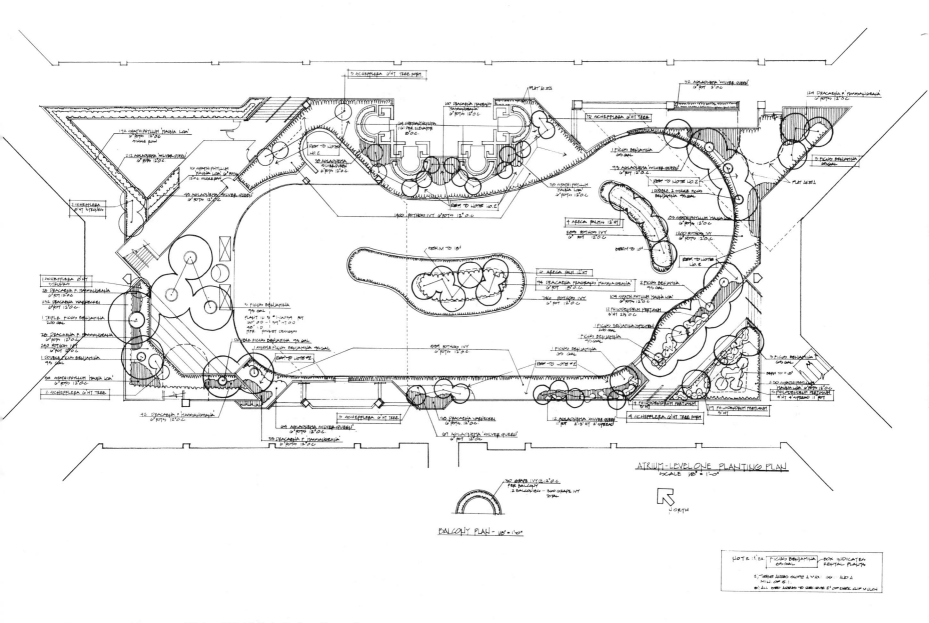

Figure 5-10. (Courtesy, Richard B. Myrick, Dallas, Texas.)

117

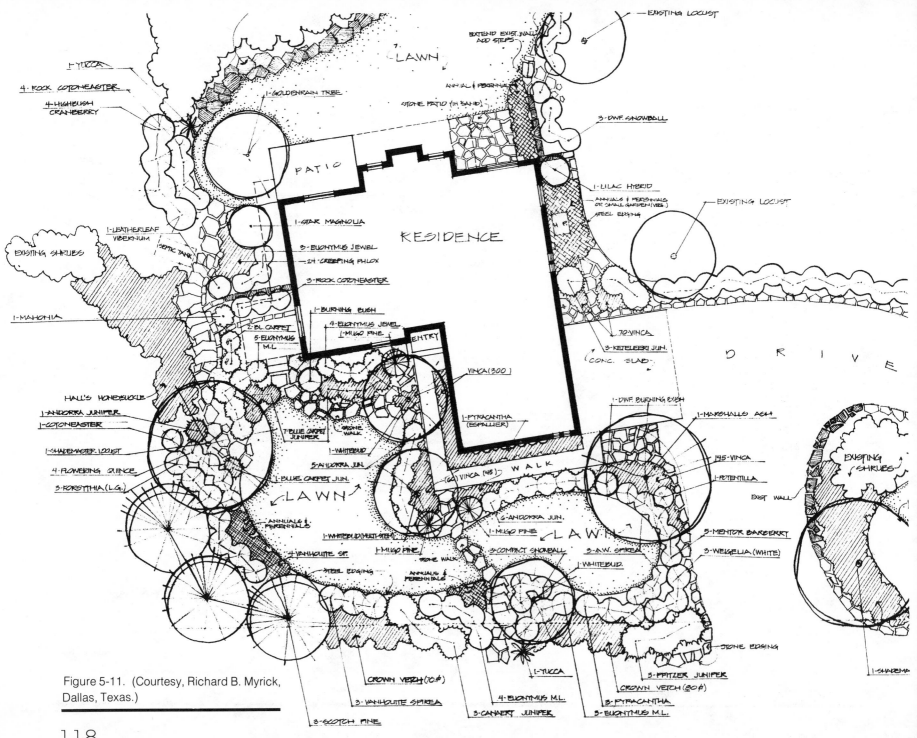

Figure 5-11. (Courtesy, Richard B. Myrick, Dallas, Texas.)

118

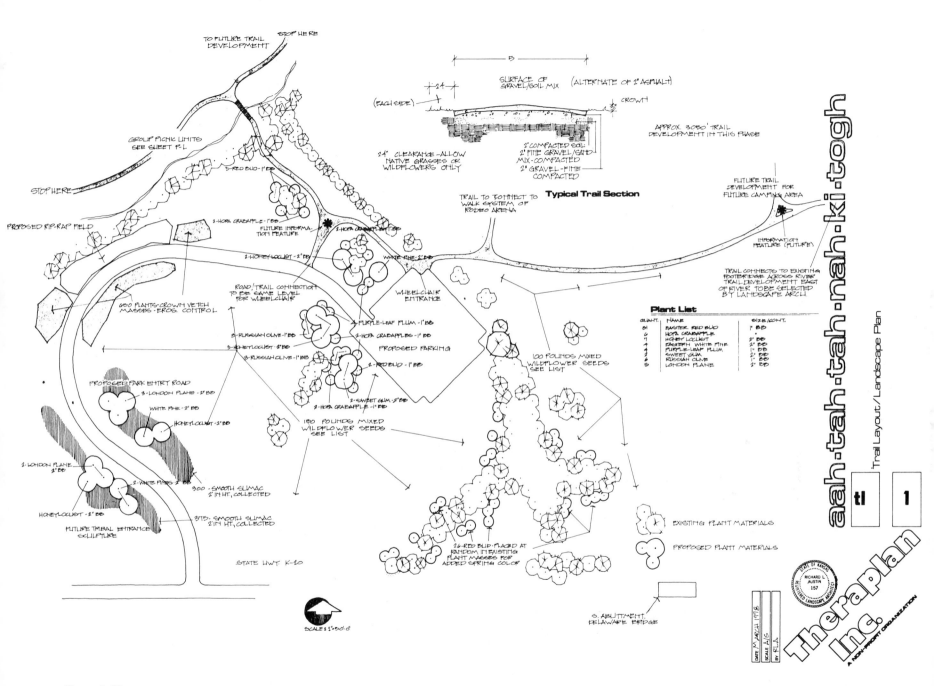

Figure 5-12.

119

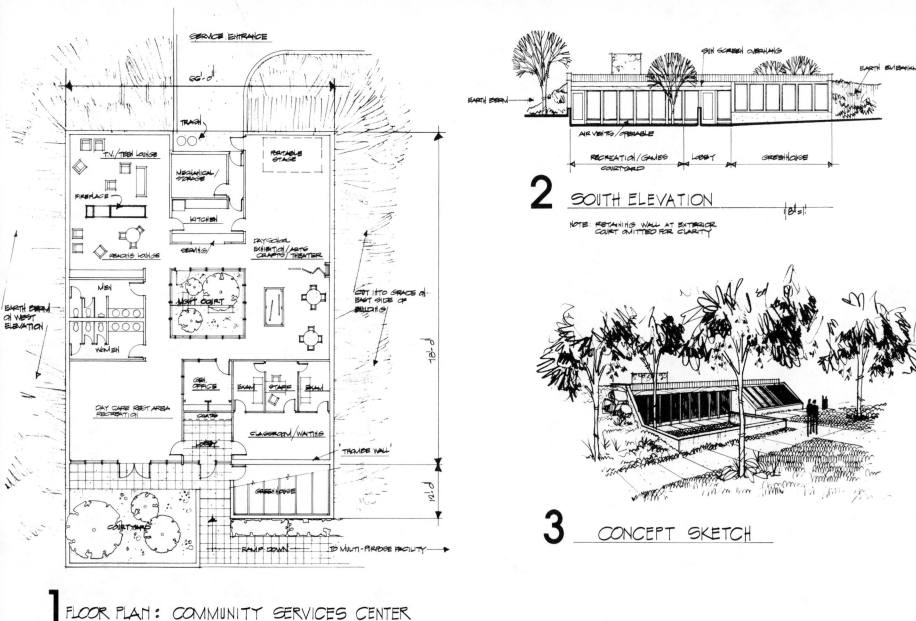

SERVICE ENTRANCE

66'-0"

TRASH

T.V./TEEN LOUNGE

MECHANICAL/ STORAGE

PORTABLE STAGE

FIREPLACE

KITCHEN

READING LOUNGE

SERVING

DAY SCHOOL EXHIBITION/ARTS CRAFTS/THEATER

MEN

NIGHT COURT

WOMEN

CUT INTO GRADE ON EAST SIDE OF BUILDING

18'-0"

DAY CARE REST AREA RECREATION

GEN. OFFICE

EXAM STAFF EXAM

EARTH BERM ON WEST ELEVATION

COATS

CLASSROOM/WAITING

LOBBY

"TROMBE WALL"

COURTYARD

GREENHOUSE

12'-0"

RAMP DOWN

TO MULTI-PURPOSE FACILITY

1 FLOOR PLAN: COMMUNITY SERVICES CENTER

APPROXIMATE FLOOR AREA - 5000 SQ. FT.   1/8"=1'-0"

2 SOUTH ELEVATION

EARTH BERM

SUN SCREEN OVERHANG

EARTH EMBANKMENT

AIR VENTS/OPERABLE

RECREATION/GAMES   LOBBY   GREENHOUSE

COURTYARD

NOTE: RETAINING WALL AT EXTERIOR COURT OMITTED FOR CLARITY

1/8"=1'

3 CONCEPT SKETCH

sdc
solar design consultants inc.
p.o. box 59128
dallas, texas 75229

IN ASSOCIATION WITH:
THERAPLAN, INC.

Figure 5-13.

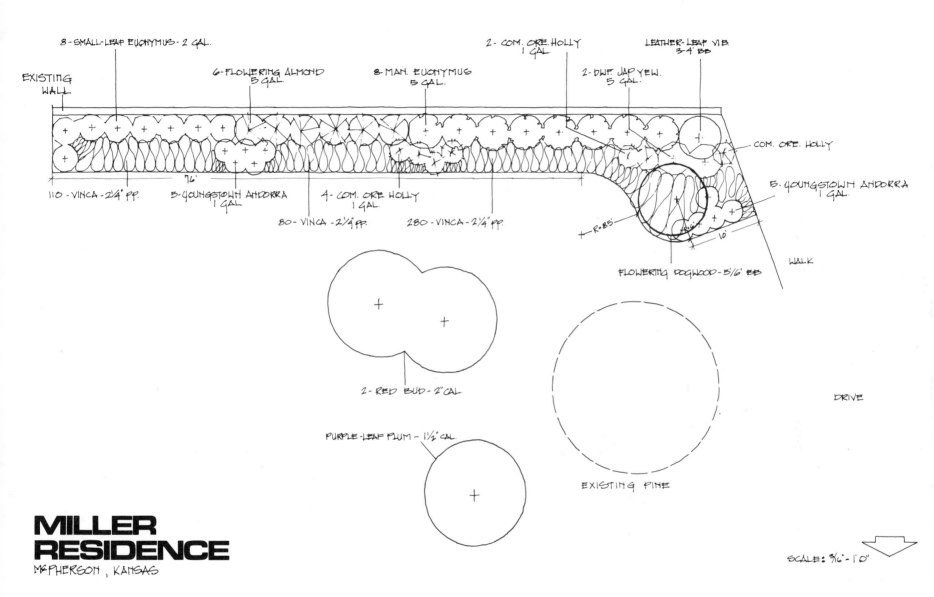

8 - SMALL-LEAF EUONYMUS - 2 GAL.

2 - COM. ORE. HOLLY
1 GAL.

LEATHER-LEAF VIB.
3-4' BB

EXISTING
WALL

6 - FLOWERING ALMOND
5 GAL.

8 - MAN. EUONYMUS
5 GAL.

2 - DWF. JAP. YEW.
5 GAL.

COM. ORE. HOLLY

110 - VINCA - 2¼" PP.

5 - YOUNGSTOWN ANDORRA
1 GAL.

4 - COM. ORE. HOLLY
1 GAL.

5 - YOUNGSTOWN ANDORRA
1 GAL.

76'

80 - VINCA - 2¼" PP.

280 - VINCA - 2¼" PP.

R-85'

10'

WALK

FLOWERING DOGWOOD - 5/6' BB

2 - RED BUD - 2" CAL.

PURPLE-LEAF PLUM - 1½" CAL.

DRIVE

EXISTING PINE

**MILLER
RESIDENCE**
McPHERSON, KANSAS

SCALE: 3/16" - 1'0"

Figure 5-14.

121

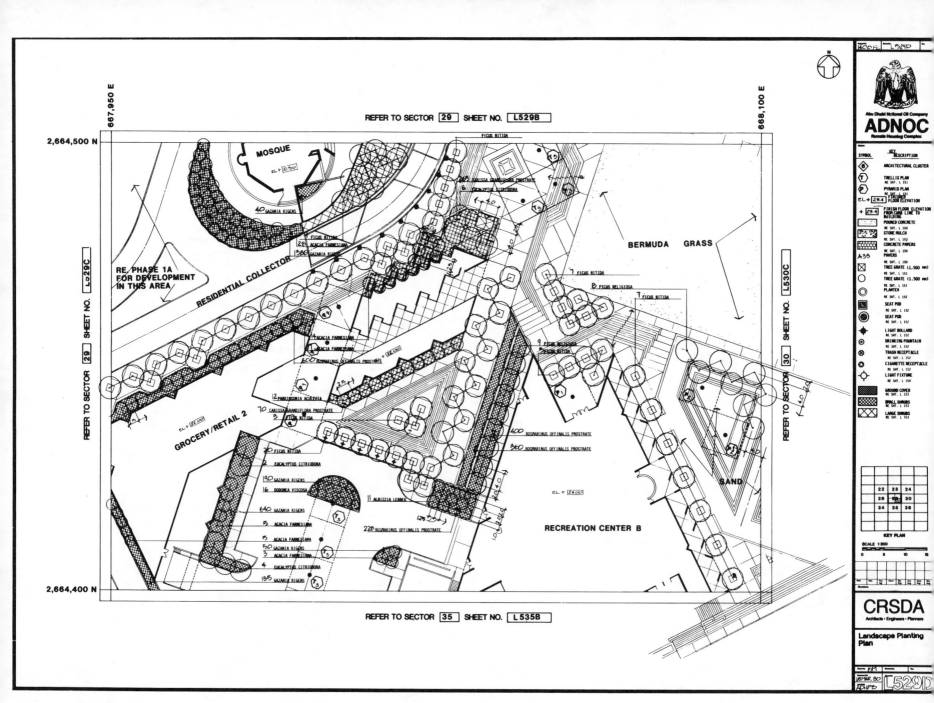

Figure 5-15. (Courtesy, Marge Edison, Manhattan, Kansas.)

GLOSSARY

Acidity: having a pH less than 7, not alkaline.

Acute: sharp, ending in a point.

Adapted: suited to particular situations.

Adventive: introduced by chance.

Aerification: cultivation or loosening of sod and topsoil for improved gas exchange.

Alkalinity: having a pH higher than 7, not acid.

Allelopathy: repressive influence by one plant upon another because of secretions or chemical influence.

Alternate: any arrangement of leaves or other parts not opposite or whorled.

Analysis, Fertilizer: percentage listing of the major nutrients.

Annual: plant that grows to maturity in one season.

Arboriculture: growing of, and caring of, trees for aesthetic purposes.

Architect: designation reserved, by law, for a person or organization professionally qualified and licensed to perform architectural services.

Asymmetrical: not alike on the two sides; "informal" design pattern.

Axis: main or central line of development of any plant or organ.

Backfill: soil replaced in an area that has been excavated previously.

Balled and Burlapped (B&B): desired amount of soil still clinging to the roots, roughly in the shape of a ball, on a plant that has been dug up out of the ground.

Bare-root Plants: plants dug out of the soil with little or no soil adhering to them.

Base Map: map indicating the significant existing physical features of a site.

Bed(s): area into which plants will be placed that has been properly prepared and treated.

Berm: continuous bank or mound of earth.

Bid: complete and properly signed proposal to do work for sums stipulated and supported by data called for by bidding requirements.

Bid Bond: bid security executed by the bidder as principal and by a surety.

Bid Date: date established for the receipt of bids.

Bid Form: form furnished to a bidder and submitted as a bid.

Bidder: person, firm, or organization that submits a bid for a contract. A bidder is not a contractor on a specific project until a contract actually exists.

Biennial: plant that requires two years in which to reach maturity.

Biodegradable: susceptible to breaking down under natural conditions.

Biomass: total organic accumulation derived from and including living organisms.

Blade: expanded part of a leaf or petal.

Broad-leaved or Broadleafs: plants having wide leaves, as compared to the narrower leaves of coniferous plants.

Building Permit: permit used by appropriate governmental authority allowing construction of a project in accordance with approved drawings and specifications.

Bush: low and thick shrub, without distinct trunk.

Caliper: diameter of a tree measured six inches above the ground if up to a four inch caliper. For a larger caliper, measurement is made twelve inches above the groundline.

Cans: containers in which plants are grown and sold.

Canning: process of planting a plant in a can or container.

Change Order: written order to the contractor, issued after the execution of the contract, authorizing a change in the project; an adjustment in the contract cost; or, the contract completion time.

Chlorosis: blanching of vegetation due to the absence of normal green chlorophyll.

Clone: group of plants originating vegetatively from the same parental source.

Clarification Drawing: graphic interpretation of the drawings or contract documents issued by the designer as part of an addendum, modification, change order, or written order.

Codes: regulations, ordinances, or legal requirements of a governmental unit which relate to the construction of a landscape project.

Compatible: material that can be used with another without counteracting or changing its effect.

Concrete Block: hollow or solid concrete masonry unit sometimes incorrectly called cementblock.

Conditioner, Fertilizer: material added to a fertilizer to prevent caking.

Conifers: plants that produce cones.

Container Plants: those that have been grown in containers as opposed to having been grown in the soil or the ground.

Contour Interval: vertical distance between adjacent contour lines.

Contour Line: line on a map or drawing that represents points of equal elevation on the ground.

Contractor: individual (or organization) that undertakes responsibility for the performance of construction work.

Cool-season Grass: species adapted to cooler climates, as opposed to species adapted to the tropics and subtropics.

Cultivar: horticulture variety.

Culvert: passage that allows for the flow of water.

Cut and Fill: process of excavating and moving the excavated material to a location as fill.

Deciduous: term that applies to plants that drop their leaves each season.

Detail: drawing indicating, in detail, the location, composition, or correlation of elements and materials shown on a larger drawing sheet.

Dormant: temporarily inactive though alive.

Ecological Niche: particular location suited to an organism.

Ecology: relationship of living things to their environment.

Ecotype: group of organisms distinguished by their ability to colonize a particular ecological niche.

Egress: exit, or means of exiting.

Eminent Domain: power or right of the nation or the state to take private property for public use.

Encroachment: unauthorized extension on the land of another.

Endemic: native to or natural, as opposed to adventive.

Epidermis: outer, protective surface layer of cells of roots, stems, or leaves.

Erosion: deterioration brought about by the abrasive action of fluids or solids in motion

Espalier: plant that has been trained to grow flat against a trellis or framework.

Evergreen Plant: plant that keeps its foliage throughout the seasons.

Excavation: removal of earth from its natural position.

Exotic: plant or other organism that has been introduced from other regions and is not native to the region to which it is introduced.

Fee: term used to denote payment for professional service.

Fern: type of flowerless plant; reproduces by spores.

Fertilizer: any natural or manufactured material added to the soil in order to supply one or more plant nutrients.

Final Acceptance: owner's acceptance of a project from the contractor upon certification by the designer that it is complete and in accordance with the contract requirements.

Footcandle: unit of illumination equal to one lumen per square foot.

Footing: portion of the foundation of a structure that transmits loads directly to the soil.

Foundation Planting: plants massed close to the foundation of a structure.

French Drain: drain consisting of a trench filled with loose stones and covered with earth. Also called boulder ditch or rubble drain.

Frond: leaf of a fern.

Full: when referring to a plant, means that it is well branched and well foliaged.

Gate Valve: flow-control device consisting of a wedge-shaped gate that can be raised to allow full, unobstructed flow or can be lowered to restrict the flow passage. Also called full-way valve.

Genus: classification unit of higher rank than species.

Germination: initiating growth or sprouting.

Gradient: degree of inclination of a surface, road, or pipe; often expressed as a percentage.

Gravity Wall: massive concrete wall that resists overturning by virtue of its own weight.

Gregarious: growing in a cluster or colony.

Ground Plane: horizontal plane of projection in a perspective drawing.

Grower: wholesale producer of nursery stock.

Grow-on: to grow a plant further until it has reached a certain desired shape or size; landscape trade term.

Growing Season: any season during which a plant is in growth.

Growth Regulator: compound capable of profoundly altering growth habits.

Guarantee: enforceable assurance of the duration of satisfactory performance or quality of product.

Habitat: environment or locale inhabited by living organisms.

Hardy Plants: those able to withstand weather conditions without special protection.

Heavy Grading: moving of large masses of earth by deep cuts and fills.

Herb: commonly, a plant used for flavoring, fragrance, or medicinal purposes.

Herbaceous: not woody; dying down each year.

Herbicide: vegetation-killing compound.

Host Plant: plant attached by, or supporting, insects or diseases.

Hybrid: plant resulting from a cross between two or more parents.

Incandescence: emission of visible light as a result of heating.

Incandescent Lamp, Incandescent Filament Lamp: lamp from which light is emitted when a tungsten filament is heated to incandescence by an electric current.

Incline: sloping surface, i.e., neither horizontal nor vertical.

Inorganic: substances occurring as minerals in nature or obtainable from them by chemical means.

Insecticide: pesticide used for controlling insects.

Inspection: examination of work completed or in progress to determine its compliance with contract requirements.

Instruction to Bidders: instructions contained in the bidding requirements for preparing and submitting bids.

Landscape Architect/Designer: person who holds a certificate to practice landscape architecture.

Landscaping: planting of plants in order to provide beauty and/or functional spaces.

Leaf Blade: expanded or flat part of a leaf.

Leaflet: one segment of a compound leaf.

Legume: nitrogen-fixing plant.

Level: surveying instrument for measuring heights with respect to an established horizontal line of sight.

Lichen: form of plant life found on rocks and other surfaces.

Lien: right enforceable against specific property to secure payment of an obligation.

Loam: soil, composed of equal parts silt and sand and less than 20% clay.

Map: graphic depiction of the surface drawn to scale.

Mechanic's Lien: lien created by statute in favor of persons supplying labor and materials for a construction project.

Microclimate: climate of a limited environs.

Microorganism: small, scarcely visible organism.

Monoculture: planting in which all plants are genetically alike.

Mulch: any loose, inert, protective material such as is used to cover new seedings.

Natural Grade: elevation of the original surface of the ground.

Natural Selection: survival of the fittest in the competition for habitat.

Nursery Stock: plants propagated and/or grown commercially.

Nutrients: elements, typically picked up through the root system, having nutritional value.

Paving Unit: any prefabricated unit used for surfacing the ground.

Pea Gravel: small-diameter natural gravel.

Peat Moss: partially or wholly decayed plant parts.

Perennial: plant that lives without end as long as the environment is favorable.

Permeability: that property of a porous material that permits the passage of water vapor.

Pesticide: chemical compound employed to kill or control pests.

pH: indication of acidity or alkalinity.

Photosynthesis: process whereby plants combine carbon dioxide and water under the auspices of chlorophyll in order to build carbohydrates.

Pinch: remove with the fingers the young growing tip of a stem or bud.

Planimeter: mechanical integrator for measuring the area of a plan surface within a given perimeter.

Plants: any kind of ornamental vegetation having a persistent woody stem or stems.

Plugging: vegetative establishment of turfgrasses in small plugs containing top growth, roots, rhizomes or stolons.

Pollination: fusion of the male reproductive cell of a plant with egg-bearing tissues.

Post-emergence: application of chemicals after crops are growing.

Potable water: water that is fit to drink.

Pots: small containers in which rooted cuttings or seedlings are planted.

Pre-emergence: application of a herbicide before the plants have emerged.

Preliminary Drawings: drawings prepared during the early stages of a project.

Propagation: production of living plants from seed or by vegetative means.

Rebar: steel bar having ribs to provide greater bonding strength when used as a reinforcing bar in concrete.

Reinforcing Bar: steel bar used in concrete construction to provide additional strength.

Reinforcing Rod: any of a variety of steel rods used in reinforced concrete.

Reinforcing Wall: wall that bears against an earth or other fill surface and resists lateral forces.

Riprap: irregularly broken and random-sized large pieces of quarry rock.

Root Ball: complete unit actually contained in the pot or container.

Rooted Cuttings: plant cuttings that have put out roots.

Rooting Aids, Rooting Compounds: chemicals that promote and hasten the rooting of cuttings.

Runner: name given to a prostrate shoot from a plant which runs along the ground.

Scalping: mowing so low as to remove most of the green foliage.

Scarification: scratching, as when slicing into the soil.

Seed Mixture: seed conglomeration containing differing species.

Shearing: practice of nonselective pruning of the surface of a plant.

Site Drainage: pipe network that conveys rainwater to a point of disposal; it is installed below grade.

Site Plan: plan of construction site that shows the position and dimensions of the project.

Slope Ratio: relation of horizontal distance to vertical rise or fall.

Soil Amendment: chemical or mineral element added to the soil to improve soil characteristics.

Soil Conditioner: material that, when added to compacted soil, tends to make it loose, crumbly, or porous.

Soil Fertility: ability of a soil to supply nutrients in sufficient quantity to meet the growth requirements of plants.

Specifications: part of the contract documents contained in the project manual consisting of written descriptions of a technical nature.

Sphagnum Moss: gray or tan bog mosses that are dried and used as a planting medium.

Splash Block: small masonry block laid on the ground below a downspout.

Spread: diameter of a plant.

Sprig: stem fragment used to propagate grasses vegetatively.

Sprigging: planting of healthy living stems of perennial turf-forming grasses.

Sticking: insertion of unrooted cuttings into the rooting medium.

Stock Plant: one from which new plants may be propagated.

Storm Drain: drain used for conveying water to a point of disposal.

Stretcher Bond, Running Bond, Stretching Bond: in masonry, a bond in which bricks or stones are laid lengthwise.

Subgrade: soil prepared and compacted to support a structure or a pavement system.

Subsoil: bed or stratum of earth that lies immediately below the surface soil.

Succession: progressive replacement of organisms in an ecological sequence until the "climax" material is attained.

Succulent: plants made drought-resistant by special water-storing powers.

Suckers: side shoot from the roots of a plant.

Surface Water: water that runs over the surface of the ground.

Surveying: branch of engineering concerned with a determination of the earth's surface features in relation to each other.

Swale: tract of low land.

Terminal: growing end of a branch or stem.

Thatch: accumulation of an undecomposed layer of dead and dying plants.

Topiary: plants formed into unusual shapes by means of extreme pruning.

Transpiration: loss of water vapor from the leaves and stems of living plants.

Tuber: short, fleshy, usually underground stem or shoot.

Variety: subdivision in a plant family.

Variegation: characteristic leaf pattern of many horticultural varieties.

Vegetative: characterized by nonreproductive asexual parts.

Vermiculite: sterile planting medium used for rooting cuttings.

Viticulture: cultivation of the grape vine.

Warm-season Grass: species adapted to tropical and subtropical environments.

Weep Hole: small opening in a wall or window member to allow for passage of water.

Wholesale Nursery: nursery that grows plants in wholesale quantities for sale at wholesale prices to the various facets of the retail nursery trade.

Wilting Point: point in decreasing soil moisture when a plant is unable to extract sufficient water for its needs, ceases to grow, and wilts.

Zoning: control by a government agency of the use of land and buildings.

Zoning Permit: permit issued by appropriate governmental authority for controlling development.

APPENDIX 1

CLIENT INTERVIEW QUESTIONNAIRE

Family Inventory
Family members: Names _____, Age _____,
Sex _____, Hobbies _____.

Public Area
Driveway _____, Number of cars in family _____.
Off-street parking needed? _____, For guests? _____.
Privacy from the street _____, Entry walk _____.
Entry garden or court _____.
Utility lighting _____, Landscape lighting _____.

Outdoor Living Area
Maintenance, how much is desired (hours) _____.
Family allergy considerations _____.
Hobby garden? _____.
Flower borders: Annuals _____, Perennials _____, Mixed _____.

Favorite plants _____,
Number of hours spent in yard/week _____.
Entertaining: Large groups _____, Small groups _____,
Formal _____, Informal _____.
Paved terrace or patio: Number of people _____,
Material _____.
Number of chairs _____, Style _____,
Number of tables_____.
Permanent seating: Benches _____, Seat-height
(walls or planters) _____.
Shade required? _____, Where _____.
Table umbrella _____, Overhead structure _____.
Area lighted? _____.
Games: What types _____.
Outdoor cooking: Permanent grill _____, Size _____,
Gas _____, Charcoal _____, Portable grill _____, Size _____.
Sink _____, Water _____, Electrical outlets _____,
Storage _____.
Swimming pool: Permanent _____, Semi-permanent _____,
Other _____, Legal Requirements _____,
Considered liability insurance _____,
Materials _____, Size _____, Lighting _____,
Shape _____.
Diving area _____, Paved decks _____, Enclosure for
pool _____, Architectural fence or wall _____,
Lighting _____, Dressing facility _____,
Equipment storage _____.

Service Area
Vegetable garden _____, Size _____.
Flower garden _____, Size _____.
Compost bin _____, Cold frames _____.
Greenhouse _____, Size _____.

Doghouse _____.

Are clotheslines necessary: Yes ____, No ____, Size _____.

Recreation vehicle storage: _____.

Lawn and garden storage _____.

Patio furniture _____.

Trash containers _____.

Children's Play Area

Sandbox _____, Slide _____, Swings _____, Ropes _____.

Playground _____, Playhouse _____.

Is shade desired _____.

Structures _____.

Should a fence be installed? Yes _____, No _____,

Height _____, Type _____.

What type of surfacing material: Sand _____, Grass _____,

Woodchips _____, Small Gravel _____,

Paved area _____.

Special features

Sculpture _____, Landscape lighting _____.

Water features: Fountain _____, Reflecting pool _____,

Fish _____, Plants _____.

Interest in birds? Bird feeder _____, Bird-attracting

plants _____, Bird bath _____, Birdhouses _____.

Site Placement

Schools:

    High School: Miles _____, Min. _____.

    Elementary: Miles _____, Min. _____.

    Kindergarten: Miles _____, Min. _____.

    Nursery: Miles _____, Min. _____.

Shopping Facilities:

    Major center: Yes _____, No _____.

    Neighborhood Store: Yes _____, No _____.

Recreation (location): Playgrounds _____, Park _____,
Swimming _____, Golf _____, Other _____.

Adjacent Structures

Note the location, size, shape, condition and possible influence site and off-site structures will have upon the design.

Utility Data

Public water supply connections: Yes _____, No _____,
Location _____.
Distance and size of the nearest main: _____.
Will this project require a private system? Yes _____,
No _____.
Subdivision plant _____.
Septic tank _____.
Individual system: _____.
Private wells: _____.
Public sewage disposal: Yes _____, No _____.
Snow removal and sanding: Yes _____, No _____.
Police protection: Yes _____, No _____.
Fire protection: Yes _____, No _____.
Storm sewers _____.
Electric service _____, Company _____.
Gas _____, Company _____.
Telephone _____, Policy on installations _____.
Street Lighting _____.
Trash collection _____.

Commercial or industrial projects

You may wish to add these questions:

1. Type of utility lighting required. Will structures, plants, or open spaces need to be illuminated?
2. Is permanent seating/outdoor furniture required? If so, where, how much, and what type?

3. What type of overhead structures (if any) are needed over seating areas, walks, entrances, or exits?
4. What type of paved surface materials are needed?
5. What type of structural enclosures are needed?
6. What type of accommodations are needed for service/maintenance equipment and supplies?
7. What type of container planting areas are desired/required for the space?
8. How much miscellaneous outdoor storage is needed/required?

APPENDIX 2

The elements used in the implementation of planting designs include a variety of contracts, special forms and planting specifications. Successful project management of a planting plan in a competitive, changing economy requires a continuous ability to adapt information and procedures from several sources to make profitable decisions. Specific forms should be developed to save processing time in the office and to insure the protection of both the designer and client.

THE SERVICE CONTRACT

This legal document establishes a specific scope of work to be performed by the planting designer. All parties involved in the program should be fully aware of each clause and a thorough definition of the project results should be outlined. Legal assistance to establish an initial contract form should be obtained because of the variations in state laws. The following sample contracts outline the minimum elements needed for a project document.

SAMPLE CONTRACT A

Date _____   Date _____

(Name) _____

(Address) _____

(City) _____

    This AGREEMENT entered into this _____ day of _____, 19_____, by and between _____(hereinafter called the "Owner") and _____(hereinafter called the "Landscape Designer/Landscape Architect").

    The Owner does hereby request the Landscape Designer/Landscape Architect to provide professional services for the landscape improvement of the property at

(Address) _____

_____.

    The professional services of the Landscape Designer/Landscape Architect shall be as follows:

A. Prepare preliminary studies of the (REAR, FRONT, ENTIRE PROPERTIES) _____to include:

    _____ TERRACE AND PATIO ADDITIONS

    _____ WALLS, RETAINING WALLS, FENCES, and/or SCREENS

    _____ PLANTING AREAS

    _____ SWIMMING POOL

    _____ CABANA

    _____ OVERHEAD STRUCTURES

    _____ GRADING and DRAINAGE PLANS

B. From preliminary studies and conferences with the Owner, a set of working drawings will be prepared to include:

POOL DESIGN and LAYOUT

PAVING AREAS

QUANTITIES, TYPE, and LOCATION OF PLANT
   MATERIALS

WALLS, SCREENS, and FENCES
LIGHTING SUGGESTIONS
BASIC PLANTING SPECIFICATIONS

The Owner agrees to pay the Landscape De-signer/Landscape Architect a fee of _____
DOLLARS upon completion of the plans and their presentation to the Owner.

The Owner shall furnish to the Landscape De-signer/Landscape Architect at the Owner's expense all neces-sary property lines, house plans, site elevations, and topo-graphic maps, applicable to the designated area to be improved. A fee of _____ DOLLARS (separate and in addition to the basic fee for design services) will be requested, if the Landscape Designer/Landscape Architect is requested to provide property and structure measurements plus site elevations.

The Landscape Designer/Landscape Architect shall furnish two sets of FINAL PRINTS upon completion to the Owner. All other prints shall be furnished at a cost of _____
_____.

Upon acceptance of the FINAL PLANS by the Owner, the Landscape Designer/Landscape Architect, at the Owner's request, may provide FULL SUPERVISION SERVICES (as opposed to DESIGN SERVICES) of all Contractors hired by the Owner to execute the LANDSCAPE PLANS for a fee of _____per hour or a lump sum of
_____ DOLLARS.

This AGREEMENT may be terminated at any time by the Owner or the Landscape Designer/Landscape Architect upon giving a thirty (30) day written notice. Upon termination at the Owner's request, payment to the Landscape

Designer/Landscape Architect shall be determined by the percentage of work completed in accordance with this AGREEMENT. This AGREEMENT, unless terminated by written notice, shall be terminated by the final payment for the finished work.

The parties hereto have executed this AGREEMENT as of the day and year first written above.

OWNER:

_____

_____

_____

LANDSCAPE
DESIGNER/LANDSCAPE
ARCHITECT

SAMPLE CONTRACT B

(Date) _____

RE: Landscape Design Services _(Project)_____
Gentlemen:

The following scope of SERVICES and AGREEMENT are presented for your authorization. It is necessary that the proper representatives of the OWNER, _____*(Owner's Name)*_____ sign and date this document and return one copy to our office.
PROCEDURE: The LANDSCAPE DESIGNER/LANDSCAPE ARCHITECT, _____*(Name)*_____, *hereby agrees to* perform the following landscape design services for _____*(Project Name)*_____, located _____, in consideration of the fees as stated in Section C-2.

A. COLLECTION OF DATA AND ON-SITE STUDY

Purpose: To acquaint the Landscape Designer/ Landscape Architect with the proposed site and examine additional planning data pertinent to the site.

Scope:

TOPOGRAPHIC MAPS
SOIL TESTS AND REPORTS
WATER AVAILABILITY AND QUALITY
ACCESS POINTS
EXISTING PLANT MATERIALS
AVAILABLE UTILITIES
PROGRAM REQUIREMENTS

Results: All reviewed data will become an integral and complementary part of the site plan. From preliminary studies, a set of working drawings will be prepared to include:

QUANTITIES, TYPE, AND LOCATION OF PLANT
MATERIAL
BASIC PLANTING SPECIFICATIONS

B. OWNER'S RESPONSIBILITY

The Owner shall provide or make available all existing data related to the work as outlined in Section A, and additional information or data which may develop during the term of this Agreement, which may possibly have a bearing on the decisions or recommendations made by the Landscape Designer/Landscape Architect. If the Owner cannot conveniently procure this information or data, then the Landscape Designer/Landscape Architect will obtain it at the Owner's expense.

Items the Owner will provide:

1. Topographic maps of the site and affected adjacent areas.

2. Architectural drawings of the site and building structures showing all areas to be affected by landscape planting.

C. FEES FOR PROFESSIONAL SERVICES

1. The fee is payable in proportion to the work completed and due upon completion of the plans and its presentation to the Owner.

2. The Owner agrees to pay the Landscape Designer/Landscape Architect a fee of _____ *(Fee)* _____ as outlined in Section A.

D. TIME OF COMPLETION

The services contracted for in Section A of this Agreement shall be completed within thirty (30) working days from the date of acceptance.

IN WITNESS WHEREOF the parties have made and executed this Agreement.

(Owner)   *(Landscape Designer/ Landscape Architect)*

By _____   By _____

Date _____   Date _____

BID PROPOSALS

Often, in a design/build operation, the service contract will be followed by a proposal to complete the features developed in the planting plan. A "bid proposal form" should also be thorough and specific for the protection of the client and designer. The one that follows is for unit pricing of a planting plan installation.

BID PROPOSAL FORM

_____ _(Date)_

Proposal of ____ _(Company Name)_ ____

_____

To: _____ _(Owner)_ _____

Gentlemen:

The Undersigned having carefully examined the Instructions to Bidders and Contract Documents comprising the Drawings and Specifications and all Documents bound therein, as prepared by and under the direction of _(Landscape Architect's name)_ and having examined the physical site of the project and being familiar with the various conditions affecting the work, the Undersigned agrees to furnish all services, labor, equipment and materials required for the performance and completion of all landscaping work as called for on the Drawings and in the Specifications for the Base Bid Lump Sum and/or sums listed below:

Base Bid for Landscaping Work ____ _(Amount in Dollars and Cents)_ ____ .

Base Bid includes all Sales Taxes, Excise Taxes, and any other taxes for all materials, appliances, and/or service subject to and upon which taxes are levied.

UNIT PRICES:

Unit prices include the cost of work and materials in place, including all materials, equipment, labor, bed preparation, fertilization, taxes, overhead, profit, maintenance and guarantee required to render the same complete. In the event a greater or lesser amount of work is done, the following unit prices will apply:

(Each plant or plant type should be listed and priced where a single tree, shrub or groundcover can be added or deducted from the project without a formal re-write of the bid.

The cost of guying and bracing should also be unit priced for each large tree and each small tree.)

ITEM	DESCRIPTION	ADD	DEDUCT
Equipment Rental		Costs Per Hour	
	Truck	_____	_____
	Tractor	_____	_____
	Tool	_____	_____
Labor Charges		Costs Per Hour	
	Foreman	_____	_____
	Common Labor	_____	_____
	Tractor Operator	_____	_____
	Truck Operator	_____	_____
Soil	(Per Yd.)	_____	_____
Tree Wrapping	(Per Tree)	_____	_____
Erosion Control Netting (if required)	(Per Sq. Yd.)	_____	_____

STARTING WORK:

The undersigned agrees that the Work to be performed under contract shall be commenced not later than _____ calendar days after the date of written notice from the Landscape Designer/Landscape Architect authorizing the Landscape Contractor to proceed with the Work.

COMPLETION DATE:

The undersigned agrees to complete the work covered by this proposal in _____ calendar days, commencing on the date construction starts.

Work shall start immediately upon awarding of a contract.

147

BID BOND:

The undersigned's Bid Security, payable to the Owner, in the form of (Cashier's Check), (Certified Check), (Bid Bond) for _____ percent of Total Sum of Bid, which 10 percent shall equal _____Dollars ($ _____).The Bid Security shall be left with the Owner in Escrow and is the measure of liquidating damages which the Owner will sustain by the failure of the undersigned to execute and deliver an Agreement and Bonds, and if undersigned defaults in executing an Agreement within _____ days of written notification of the Award of the Contract to him or in furnishing any required bonds within _____ days thereafter then the Bid Security shall become the property of the Owner, but if this proposal is not accepted within _____ days of the date set for the submission of bids, or if the undersigned executes and delivers said Contract and required Bonds, the Bid Security shall be returned to him or receipt thereof.

PERFORMANCE BOND AND LABOR AND MATERIAL BOND

The undersigned agrees, if awarded the Contract, to execute and deliver to the Owner, within _____ days after signing the Contract, a Performance Bond and Labor and Material Payment Bond, signed by himself as principal and by an established reputable bonding or insurance company (satisfactory to the Owner) or surety on the forms as specified in the penal sum of 100% of the Contract Price, on each Performance and Payment Bond. Such bonds shall remain in full force and effect from the date of signing the Contract until the acceptance of the Work by the Owner. The Contractor shall promptly file a signed copy of the Contract and the Performance Bond and Labor and Material Payment Bond with the County Clerk's office in full compliance with the law.

The undersigned agrees to purchase and furnish Performance and Payment Bonds for the Total Sum of: _____

_____Dollars ($_____).

INSURANCE:

   The undersigned agrees, if awarded the Contract, to deliver to the Owner, within _____ days after the date of written notice to proceed with the Work and before proceeding with any Work the Certificates of Insurance as specified.

   Name of the Insurance Company used by this Bidder:

_____.

TAXES:

   The above prices include all applicable taxes, insurance, benefits, overhead and profit.

   Bidder understands that the Owner reserves the right to reject any or all bids and to waive any informalities in the bidding.

   The bidder agrees that this bid shall be good and may not be withdrawn within _____ days after the actual date of the opening thereof.

                    Respectfully submitted,
                    (Company Name) _____
                    By _____
                    Title _____
                    Address _____
                          _____
                    Telephone _____

PLANTING SPECIFICATIONS

The specifications a designer uses will determine the success or failure of a planting project, for it is the specifications document that sets forth the protective measures and communication elements that allow a third party to construct the creations of the designer. Whether an in-house process for a design/build operation or a competitive bid for a public installation, the following sample specifications will illustrate the important components needed for this document.

SAMPLE INSTRUCTIONS TO BIDDERS

A. Preparation and Submission of Bid

    1. Bids shall be submitted to _____ (Owner) and shall be signed in ink. Erasures or other changes in a bid must be explained, or noted over the signature of the Bidder. Bids shall not contain any conditions, omissions, unexplained erasures or items not called for in the proposal, or irregularities of any kind.

    2. Each bid must give the full business address of the bidder and be signed by an authorized representative. Bids by partnerships must furnish the full name of all partners and must be signed in the partnership name by one of the members of the partnership, or by an authorized representative, followed by the signature and designation of the person signing. Bids by corporations must be signed with the legal name of the corporation, followed by the signature and designation of the President, Secretary, or other persons authorized to bind it in the matter. The name of each person signing shall also be typed or printed below the signature. A bid by a person who affixed to his signature "President," "Secretary," "Agent," or other designation, without disclosing the principal, may be held to be the bid of the individual signing.

    3. Bids shall be in sealed envelopes which shall have marked on the outside the following: _____
_____*(State How Addressed and How Coded)*_____.
If forwarded by mail, the sealed envelope containing the bid must be enclosed in another envelope addressed as specified above.

B. Modification and Withdrawal of Bids

1. Telegraph bids will not be considered, but modifications by telegraph or letter of bids already submitted will be considered, if received prior to the hour set for opening.

2. Bids may be withdrawn by written or telegraphic request received from bidders prior to the time fixed for opening.

3. Two signed copies of the telegram should be forwarded immediately to the office, in a sealed envelope, to which the written bid was submitted.

C. Examination of Plans and Sites

1. The Bidders shall carefully examine the plans and specifications to fully understand the location, extent, nature, and amount of work to be performed.

2. Each Bidder shall visit the site of the proposed work and thoroughly acquaint himself with conditions relating to the work.

D. Rejection of Bids

1. The competency and responsibility of Bidders will be considered in making the award.

2. The Owner or duly appointed representative reserves the right to reject any or all bids, and to waive any informality in bids received.

E. Specifications and Drawings

1. Specifications are intended to be complementary, and anything mentioned in the specifications and not shown on the plans, or shown on the plans and not mentioned in the specifications, shall be of like effect as if shown or mentioned in both. In the event of conflict between the drawings and specifications, it shall be brought to the attention of the Landscape Architect or Landscape Designer immediately for clarification.

2. Omissions from the plans or specifications, or the misdescription of details of work which are evidently necessary to

carry out the intent of the plans and specifications, which are customarily performed, shall not relieve the Bidder/Contractor from performing such omissions and details or work, but they shall be performed as if fully and correctly set forth and described in the plans and specifications.

3. The Bidder/Contractor shall check all plans and specifications furnished to same, immediately upon their receipt, and shall promptly notify the Landscape Architect or Landscape Designer of any discrepancies therein.

4. If any discrepancies are brought to the attention of the Landscape Architect or Landscape Designer, he/she will notify and send written instructions to all Bidders.

5. The Bidder's/Contractor's authorized representative shall have a set of plans (with omissions, ambiguities, or discrepancies on the plans) with him/her on the site. During the course of the work, should any errors, omissions, ambiguities, or discrepancies be found on the plans or in the specifications, or should there be found any discrepancies between the plans and specifications to which the Contractor has failed to call attention before submitting the bid, then the Owner will interpret the intent of the plans and specifications, and the Bidder/Contractor shall abide by the Owner's interpretation and shall carry out the work in accordance with the decision of the Owner. The Owner may interpret or construe the plans and specifications as to secure, in all cases, the most substantial and complete performance of the work as is consistent with the needs and requirements of the work.

6. Laws and regulations. The Bidder's attention is directed to the fact that applicable state laws, municipal ordinances, and the rules and regulations of all authorities having jurisdiction over construction of the project shall apply to the contract throughout, and they will be deemed to be included in the contract the same though herein written out in full.

7. Insurance. The Contractor, before starting work on the project, must furnish to the Owner a "Certificate of Insurance" or other acceptable evidences from a reputable insurance company or companies licensed to write insurance in the State of _____, showing that the Contractor is covered by insurance as follows:

    (a) Workmen's Compensation Insurance

    (b) Contractor's and Subcontractor's Public Liability and Property Damage Insurance

Insurance as above stipulated must be maintained throughout the period of time required for construction and until the work is accepted. The certificates or evidences of insurance shall be set forth that the Insurance Carrier will notify the Owner in the event such insurance is cancelled or terminated prior to acceptance of the work.

8. Contractor's cooperation. Bidder's attention is called to the fact that there may be other Prime Contractors working on the project and it is expected that the bidder/contractor will cooperate to expedite all phases of construction.

9. The Contractor will be furnished two copies of the plans and one copy of the specifications. If necessary, extra copies of the plans and/or specifications will be furnished at Owner's expense.

SAMPLE SPECIFICATIONS

Specifications for _(Name of Job, Job Number)_

Job Locations _(Street Number, City or Town)_

  I. Scope of Work

    Extent: In general the item of work to be performed under this section shall include, but is not limited to:

      All materials, equipment, tools, transportation, services, and labor required for the complete installation:

1. Lawn construction
2. Planting of trees
3. Protection, maintenance, and replacement of lawns and trees and all related items necessary to complete the work indicated on the drawings and/or specified herein.

II. Plant Materials

A. Plant list: The Contractor shall furnish and plant all plants shown on the drawings, as specified, and in quantities listed on the plant materials list. A list of plants is shown on the planting plan and at the end of these specifications.

B. Quality and size: Plants shall have a habit of growth that is normal for the species and shall be sound, healthy, vigorous, and free from insect pests. They shall be equal to or exceed the measurements specified in the Plant List, which are minimum acceptable sizes. They shall be measured before pruning, with branches in normal position. Any necessary pruning shall be done at time of planting. Requirements for measurements, branching, and grading quality of plants in the Plant List generally follow the code of standards currently recommended by the American Association of Nurserymen, Inc., in the American Standard for Nursery Stock. The Owner shall have the option to select and tag any or all plants at the Nursery prior to delivery to the job site. When plants at a specified kind or size are not available within a reasonable distance, substitutions may be made upon request by the Contractor, if approved by the Owner or his representative. All plants shall conform to the measurements specified in their Plant List. Exceptions are as follows:

1. Plants larger than specified in the plant list may be used if approved by the Owner or his representative, but use of such plants shall not increase the contract price. If the use of larger plants is approved, the spread of root or ball of earth shall be increased in proportion to the size of the plant.

2. Up to 10% of undersized plants in any one variety of grade may be used provided that there are sufficient plants above size to make the average equal to or above specified grade and provided that undersized plants are larger than the average size of the next smaller grade.

C. Type of protection to roots:

1. Balled and burlapped plants: Plants designated B&B in the Plant List shall be balled and burlapped. They shall be dug with firm, natural balls of earth of sufficient diameter and depth to encompass the fibrous and feeding root system necessary to full recovery of the plant. Balls should be firmly wrapped with burlap or similar materials and bound with twine cord or wire mesh.

2. Container grown plants: Plants grown in containers will be accepted as B & B, provided that the plant had been growing in the container for "one full growing season" prior to delivery.

3. Protection after delivery: The balls of "B & B" plants that cannot be planted immediately on delivery shall be covered with moist soil or mulch, or other protection from drying winds and sun. All plants shall be watered as necessary until planted.

III. Materials (Other than Plants)

A. Topsoil to be furnished: If the quantity of excavated topsoil is inadequate (as determined by the Landscape Architect or Landscape Designer) for planting purposes, the sufficient additional topsoil shall be furnished on the site by the _____ *(Bidder or Owner)*

B. Commercial fertilizer: Commercial fertilizer shall be an organic fertilizer containing the following minimum percentage of available plant food by weight: N _____ P _____ K _____. Mixed nitrogen—not less than *(Percent)* from organic source. Inorganic chemical nitrogen shall not be derived from the sodium form of nitrate or from ammonia nitrate. It shall be delivered to the site in unopened original containers, each bearing the manufacturer's guaranteed analysis. Any fertilizer that becomes caked or otherwise damaged, making it unsuitable for use, will not be accepted.

C. Water: Water shall be suitable for irrigation and free from ingredients harmful to plant life. The Contractor will furnish hoses and watering equipment required for work. Water for work will be furnished by Owner.

D. Sod: Sod shall contain a good cover of living or growing grass. At least _____% of the plants in the sod shall be composed of _____ *(Name)* _____. The sod shall be freshly dug, well rooted, and relatively free from weeds or undesirable plants, and it shall be entirely free of Nut Grass, large stones, roots, and other material that might be detrimental to the development of the sod. It shall be of uniform thickness with a minimum _____ inch thickness of soil and roots.

E. Grass seed: Grass seed shall be of kind named, harvested within one year prior to planting, free of weeds, to the limits allowable under applicable State seed laws. The seed shall be hulled and have a germination and purity that will produce a pure live-seed content of not less than 75%.

F. Anti-desiccant (optional): Anti-desiccant shall be "Wilt Pruf" or equal, delivered in manufacturer's containers and used according to the manufacturer's instructions.

G. Mulch: Mulch shall be wood chips, ground bark, bark peelings, peat, hay or straw, salt marsh hay, sugar cane, ground corn cobs, or peanut hulls.

IV. Protection of Existing Trees

A. Before beginning any clearing work and before beginning any excavation or stripping work the Contractor shall consult with the designer on the selection and protection of all existing trees designated on the drawings and/or marked to remain on the site.

B. Tree protection shall consist of a fence of a minimum 5-foot height, sturdy and approved construction, utilizing cedar or wood fence posts with 2" x 4" stringers at the top and bottom, and 1" x 6" vertical boards spaced 9 inches on centers. The fence shall be constructed a minimum distance of 5 feet from the outer trunks.

C. All such fencing shall be maintained throughout the work under this Contract until such time as the area is ready for lawns and planting work, at which time it shall be removed and disposed of by the Contractor.

D. The fenced areas shall not be used for storage or materials of any kind or for any purpose likely to damage tree roots or branches. Repair injuries to bark, trunk and branches of fenced trees (if required) by dressing, cutting, and painting as directed by the Landscape Architect/Landscape Designer.

E. For any tree designated to remain that is removed or damaged to the extent that it will not live, or damaged to the extent it cannot be used in the landscape development, as determined by the Landscape Architect/Landscape Designer the Contractor shall replace the tree with another of equivalent size, as selected by the Landscape Architect/Landscape Designer and at no cost to the Owner.

V. Removal of Trees

Trees designated to be removed on plans shall be grubbed out _____ feet below natural ground to include all main roots and the cutting of the tap root, and said trees shall be removed from the site.

VI. Installation (General)

A. Seasons for planting: Planting may be done whenever the weather and soil conditions are favorable or as otherwise authorized by the Owner or his representative and with the consent of the Contractor.

B. Planting tree pit size: Minimum diameter (width) and depth of planting pits for balled and burlapped, bare root and container grown plants shall be as follows:
   1. Pit diameter: _____ inches greater than diameter of ball or spread of roots.
   2. Pit depth: _____ inches greater than depth of ball or roots.

C. Preparation of planting areas: Before excavations are made, the surrounding turf shall be covered in a manner that will satisfactorily protect all turfed areas that are to be trucked over, and upon which soil is to be temporarily stacked pending its removal or reuse as specified herein. Existing trees, shrubbery, and beds that are to be preserved shall be barricaded in a manner that will effectively protect them during the planting operations.

D. Setting plants: Unless otherwise specified, all plants shall be planted in pits, centered, and set on prepared soil to such depth that the finished grade level at the plant after settlement will be the same as that at which the plant was grown. They shall be planted upright and faced to give the best appearance or relationship to adjacent structures. No burlap shall be pulled from under the balls. Platform wire, and surplus binding from top and sides of the balls shall be removed. All broken or frayed roots shall be cut off cleanly. Prepared soil shall be placed and compacted carefully to avoid injury to roots and to fill all voids. When the hole is nearly filled, add water as necessary and allow it to soak away. Fill the hole to finished grade, allowing for 2 inches of mulch, and form a shallow saucer around each plant by placing a ridge of topsoil around the edge of each pit. Remove containers after planting.

E. Staking, wrapping, guying and anchoring of trees:

1. Space trees uniformly as indicated and set trees plumb, straight, at such a level that, after settlement, normal or natural relationship of plant crown with ground surface will be established. To accomplish this remove platforms, wire, and binding from top and sides of balls, but do not remove burlap under balls; and fill pits around trees to finish grade, thoroughly soak and repeat filling until all settlement has taken place, allowing 2 inches for mulch at grade and forming a circular dam of top soil around edge of each pit.

2. All trees shall be properly staked, wrapped with burlap from base to first branches, and guyed.

F. Mulching: Trees shall be mulched within 2 days after planting by covering the entire beds or pits with a 2-inch deep layer of a material specified by the Landscape Architect/Landscape Designer; mulch shall be thoroughly saturated with water after placing to prevent displacement by wind and water.

G. Excess excavated soil (optional): Excess excavated soil shall be disposed of on or off the site directed by the Owner.

H. Grass areas: Plant grass in all areas within limits of entire project site, except areas indicated or specified to be developed otherwise, as follows:

1. *(Name)* Grass: This shall be planted within a project boundary between curbs, walks, and buildings.

2. Grades: The areas to be spot-sodded or seeded, as established by others, shall be maintained in a true, even, and properly compacted condition so as to prevent the formation of depressions where water will stand. All areas with the grade equal to or greater than 2 to 1 shall receive solid sodding.

3. Tilling: Before any sod is planted, the areas to be planted to grass shall be thoroughly tilled to a minimum depth of 3 inches by plowing, disking, harrowing, rototilling, or other approved operations until the condition of the soil is friable and of uniform texture. The work shall be performed only during the period when beneficial results are likely to be obtained. Any irregularities in the surface of finish grades, resulting from tillage or other operations, shall be leveled out before sodding operations are begun. All stones, bricks, roots, or similar

substances of 1½ inches or more in diameter, resulting from tillage, shall be removed and disposed of off the site.

4. Laying of sod: Before any sod is laid, all soft spots and inequalities in grade shall be corrected. Grass sod blocks for spot sodding shall be _____ inches square. The blocks shall be planted uniformly _____ inches apart (from the center of the block). After excavation for the block but before setting the block in place, a small amount of fertilizer shall be placed under each block of sod. Then blocks are to be planted, foliage side up, to a depth of the finished-lawn grade and soil firmly placed around them. Then they shall be evenly fertilized with a mechanical spreader at the rate of _____ pounds per 1,000 square feet of area. Fertilizer shall be commercial fertilizer as specified. On completion of the fertilizing, the areas shall be rolled with a _____ pound roller and the completed, sodded surface shall be even and true to finish grade.

5. Sowing of the grass seed:
   a. Fertilizing: Prior to tilling areas to be planted with grass seed, supply _(Number of Pounds)_ commercial fertilizer at the rate of _____ pounds per acre of lawn area being prepared for seeding.
   b. Scarifying: Within 24 hours following fertilizer application and before any seed is sown, scarify the ground to be seeded, as necessary, until surface is smooth, friable, and of uniformly fine texture.

c. Seeding: Seed lawn areas evenly with mechanical spreader at rate of _____ pounds per acre. Sow half of the seeds with a sower, moving at right angles to first sowing. *Do Not* broadcase seeding in windy weather. The Contractor must assume full responsibility for establishing smooth, uniformly covered grass lawn.

6. Watering: Water shall be applied to sodded areas in quantities and at intervals to provide optimum growing conditions for the establishment of a healthy, uniform stand and cover of grass. Apply water by use of hose and attached sprinklers, soaker hose, or other watering equipment that will apply water at such rate as to avoid damage to finished surfaces.

I. Obstructions below ground: In the event that rock or underground construction work or obstructions are encountered in any plant pit excavation work to be done under this contract, alternate locations shall be selected by the Owner and the Landscape Contractor. The Landscape Contractor shall be paid for the removal of such rock or underground obstructions encountered at a rate per cubic yard to be agreed upon by the Owner's representative and the Landscape Contractor.

J. Planting operations:

1. Time of planting: The Contractor shall be notified by the Owner, when other divisions of the work have progressed sufficiently, to commence work on lawns and planting Thereafter planting operations during the next season or seasons that are normal for such work as determined by accepted practice in the locality of the project. At the option,

and on the full responsibility of the General Contractor, planting operations may be conducted under unseasonable conditions without additional compensation.

2. Layout: The locations for plants and outlines of areas to be planted, as indicated on the plan, shall be marked on the ground by the General Contractor before any excavation is made. All such locations shall be approved by the Owner and the Landscape Architect/Landscape Designer or Contractor. Where construction or utilities, below ground or overhead, are encountered or where changes have been made in the construction, necessary adjustments will be approved by the Owner. Plants shall be a minimum of _(distance)_ from buldings.

3. Pruning and repair: Upon completion of the work under this Contract, all existing trees and shrubs shall have been pruned and any injuries repaired. The amount of pruning shall be limited to the minimum necessary to remove dead or injured twigs or branches that interfere with new construction (buildings, roof, overhang, fences, etc.). Pruning shall be done in such a manner as not to change the natural habit or shape of the plant. All cuts shall be made flush, leaving no stubs. On all cuts over ¾ inch in diameter, bruises, or scars on the bark, the injured cambium shall be traced back to living tissue and removed; wood shall be smoothed and shaped so as not to retain water; and the treated areas shall be coated with a tree paint, as approved by the Landscape Architect/Landscape Designer.

VII. Maintenance

    A. Grass lawn areas: Grass spot sodding and sodded lawn areas shall be protected and maintained by watering, mowing, and replanting as necessary for at least _____ days after completion of all spot sodding and acceptance. Scattered bare spots, none of which shall be larger than 4 square feet, will be allowed to a maximum of 3 percent of any lawn area. Correct all depressions where water will stand.

    B. Grass lawn areas: Grass seeded lawn areas shall be protected and maintained as necessary for at least _____ days after completion of all seeding. Maintenance shall include watering, repairing any damage that has occurred to the seeded areas from erosion, mowing of weeds (when height of weeds interferes with seedlings), and reseeding as originally specified any areas where a good stand of grass is not obtained.

    C. Other planting protection and maintenance: All trees are to be protected and maintained until the end of the maintenance period. Maintenance shall include watering, weeding, cultivating, removing dead material, resetting plants to proper grades or upright position, restoring the planting saucer, and other necessary operations. If planting is done after lawn preparation, properly protect lawn areas and repair any damage resulting from planting operations promptly.

VIII. Guarantee Periods

Plants shall be guaranteed by the Landscape Contractor from one planting season to the first of the following planting season.

IX. Inspection and Provisional Acceptance

A. The Owner or his/her representative shall inspect all work for provisional acceptance upon the written request of the Contractor. The request shall be received at least 10 days before the anticipated date of provisional inspection.

B. Upon completion of all repairs or replacements that may appear at the time of the inspection to be necessary (in the judgment of the Owner and the Landscape Contractor), the Owner shall certify in writing to the Landscape Contractor as to the provisional acceptance of the planting items.

C. The Owner shall pay, or cause to be paid, to the said Landscape Contractor a sum of money to be not less than 90% of the total cost planting due the said Landscape Contractor.

X. Final Inspection and Final Acceptance

A. At the end of the guarantee period, inspection of plants will be made by the Owner or his representative upon written notice requesting such inspection, submitted by the Landscape Contractor at least 10 days before the anticipated date of inspection.

B. Any plant, as required under this contract, that is dead, not true to name or size as specified, or not in satisfactory growth, as determined by the Owner and the Landscape Contractor, shall be removed from the site.

XI. Application for Payments

A. Performance under this contract will be subject to approval or disapproval by: *(Landscape Architect*/Landscape Designer).

B. No later than the first and fifteenth day of each calendar month, if a certified estimate has been received 10 days prior to date of payment, the Owner will make partial payment to the Contractor on the basis of a duly certified approved estimate of the work performed during the preceding semi-monthly period by the Contractor. The Owner will retain 10% of the amount of each such estimate until no later than 30 working days after final completion and final acceptance of all work covered by the contract.

XII. Clean Up

Any soil, peat, or similar material that has been brought on to paved areas by hauling or other operations shall be removed promptly by the Landscape Contractor, keeping these areas clean at all times. Upon completion of planting, all excess soil, stones, and debris that have not previously been cleaned up shall be removed from the site or disposed of as directed by the Owner. All lawns and planting areas shall be prepared for final inspection.

FACTORS INFLUENCING COSTS

Some requirements written into specifications will cause the final project cost to vary, based upon local conditions at the time of planting. The designer should be aware of these requirements and be prepared to adjust the plan accordingly.

1. *The Retail Cost of Plant Materials:* Often the retail cost will act as a guide for determining a base price for installation. Some construction firms use their wholesale price and multiply this cost by a factor of 2.5, 3.3 or 4.0. Other firms use the wholesale cost of materials, add their labor costs, and then multiply with an overhead percentage. Be careful specifying which technique is allowable. It may be best to leave it to the discretion of the bidding firm to insure a competitive submission.

2. *Mulching:* If more than the required peat mulch is used, costs could expand proportionally to the availability of the desired material.

3. *Tree Staking, Wrapping and Guying:* Make sure each of these items are needed for the specified material. Requiring trees under 2″ in caliper to be staked, wrapped and supported with wires may be a waste of time and materials.

4. *Material Guarantee:* In some geographic areas, a guarantee of more than sixty to ninety days may add as much as ten to fifteen percent to the base price. Most plants will wilt and die during the first ninety days if they are of inferior quality.

5. *Maintenance:* Reasonable maintenance time of thirty days will add to the base price only slightly. It is always good to have a well maintained project for a long period after construction, but the installation contractor will add these costs to an already inflated base price.

6. *Length of Project:* Make sure a reasonable time is allowed to complete the installation. The designer should take into consideration the factors of material availability, labor, and transportation to the site before committing to a specific time.

7. *Special Size or Conditions Materials:* A unique plant or material specimen is always an attractive addition to any landscape space, but remember, it is more expensive and should be budgeted accordingly—usually three to four times as much as a typical specimen.

8. *Special Planting Seasons:* Careful attention should be paid to the time of the year required for the planting operation. Some weather seasons require additional expenditures for planting techniques and material protection. These costs, with overhead percentages, will be passed along to your client.

FIELD CONSIDERATIONS FOR PLANTING DEVELOPMENTS

After the planting plan has been completed and the specifications written, the responsibility of the designer should be directed to the inspection phases of the project. Essentially, there are three phases of an operation that may require the inspection services of the designer: first, before formal planting begins; second, during the planting operations; and third, the final inspection upon completion.

PRE-PLANTING INSPECTION

Part IX of the *Planting Specifications* sets forth the conditions of the plant materials to be used in a project. For some designers, an inspection prior to the formal spec writing is used to determine existing conditions and availability of desired material. Other designers prefer to inspect the materials after the formal writing. Both inspections are usually completed at a nursery or garden center and offer a reasonable amount of quality control.

A good designer, however, maintains an on-going inspection program of local nurseries and growing operations to secure a competent knowledge of trade conditions and consumer trends. It is best to know "what is available" and "where you can get it" before entering a planting design program. Many of the most comprehensive and creative plans have been placed on a shelf because the designer used "nonexistent" plant material.

In a pre-planting inspection, you should study the general condition of the plants and look specifically at the following:

1. *Foliage Color:* Discoloration of foliage indicates several problems—from poor drainage to disease.
2. *Growth Uniformity:* If a specific plant size is needed, make

sure all species in the needed size are uniform in growth quality.

3. *Condition:* Inspect the plants to make sure they are disease and pest-free as well as void of any damage from pruning or ice storms.

PLANTING INSPECTION

This phase will insure the proper use of techniques suitable to local climate and trade conditions. The first step in this phase actually begins when the plants arrive at the site. If the material has not been tagged (for representative samples) prior to delivery, the designer should check for any discoloration of foliage, uniformity of plant growth, and general condition of each plant.

Additional inspection steps for this phase should include:

1. *Bed Preparation:* Check for uniformity of depth, soil mix, and tillage.
2. *Pit or Pocket Excavation:* There should be uniformity in excavation, location, etc.
3. *General Site Preparation:* Uniformity of grade, tillage, or topsoil depth should be checked.
4. *Location/Spacing of Plants:* Tagging or staking for trees, shrubs, and groundcovers may be required.
5. *Plant Protection:* During the interim period, check the storage conditions for the plants. If wrapping, staking and pruning is required, check to see if the workmanship is proper.

FINAL INSPECTION AFTER PLANTING

The last phase of an inspection program is governed by the specifications. The more detailed the requirements, the more detailed the final inspection will be. An "inspection checklist," taken from the specifications, should be developed for this inspection— and strictly followed.

DETERMINING MAINTENANCE IMPACT

The true success or failure of a planting composition will be determined by the level of effort and care taken to perpetuate the designers' original objectives. The amount of enclosure of the walls, the attractiveness of accents, and the shapes of the original forms are important if the images of the space are to remain. Why spend many hours for research and design if you plan to simply walk away from a project after the final inspection.

In order to complete this important aspect of the design program, the planting designer must develop a maintenance impact statement. A statement, or a plan of action, to determine the amount and type of care to be taken to insure the continuation of the composition theme. The minimal requirements for such a plan should include:

1. *Description of the projected levels of service* needed to maintain the composition: This should include *all* forms of minimum maintenance for the plants (i.e., watering, weeding, mowing, clipping, etc.).
2. *Estimated annual and seasonal costs* to reach the minimum maintenance levels: This should include equipment, energy, supplies, and vandalism.
3. *The dates of the maintenance services* for each season of the year, plus special programs for special services.

There are numerous reference materials available for determining what must be done to insure the growth and development of the plants chosen for a composition. The designer may even wish to add a maintenance specialist to the planning team to assist in the completion of a total service program.

APPENDIX 3

REFERENCE GUIDES FOR IMPLEMENTATION

The following tables and details can be used for making the necessary estimates and computations for a planting plan installation.

DIAMETER OF PLANTING BALL FOR SHADE TREES (RECOMMENDED)

Caliper* (in.)	Minimum Diameter	Minimum Depth
1½−1½	18″ (45.72 cm)	13.5″ (34.29 cm)
1½−1¾	20″ (50.80 cm)	13.3″ (33.78 cm)
1¾−2	22″ (55.88 cm)	14.7″ (37.34 cm)
2 −2½	24″ (60.96 cm)	16″ (40.64 cm)
2½−3	28″ (71.12 cm)	18.7″ (47.50 cm)
3 −3½	32″ (81.28 cm)	19.2″ (48.77 cm)
3½−4	38″ (96.52 cm)	22.8″ (57.91 cm)
4 −4½	42″ (106.68 cm)	25.2″ (64.00 cm)
4½−5	46″ (116.84 cm)	27.6″ (70.10 cm)
5 −5½	54″ (137.16 cm)	32.4″ (82.30 cm)

*Horticultural Determination

BARE ROOT TREES — SPREAD OF ROOTS FOR PLANTING (RECOMMENDED)

Caliper* (in.)	Height	Root Spread
½– ¾	5– 6′ (1.53–1.83m)	12″ (30.48 cm)
¾–1	6– 8′ (1.83–2.44m)	16″ (40.64 cm)
1 –1¼	7– 9′ (2.13–2.74m)	18″ (45.72 cm)
1¼–1½	8–10′ (2.44–3.05m)	20″ (50.80 cm)
1½–1¾	10–12′ (3.05–3.66m)	22″ (55.88 cm)
1¾–2	10–12′ (3.05–3.66m)	24″ (60.96 cm)
2 –2½	12–14′ (3.66–4.27m)	28″ (71.12 cm)
2½–3	12–14′ (3.66–4.27m)	32″ (81.28 cm)
3 –3½	14–16′ (4.27–4.88m)	38″ (96.52 cm)

*Horticultural Determination

HEIGHT RELATIONSHIP TO CALIPER

Caliper* (in.)	Height
½– ¾	5– 6′ (1.53–1.83m)
¾–1	6– 8′ (1.83–2.44m)
1 –1½	7– 9′ (2.13–2.74m)
1½–1¾	10–12′ (3.05–3.66m)
1¾–2	10–12′ (3.05–3.66m)
2 –2½	12–14′ (3.66–4.27m)
2½–3	12–14′ (3.66–4.27m)
3 –3½	14–16′ (4.27–4.88m)
3½–4	14–16′ (4.27–4.88m)
4 –5	16–18′ (4.88–5.49m)
5 –6	18′ (5.49m) and up

*Horticultural Determination

PLANTING PIT REQUIREMENTS — B&B STOCK (RECOMMENDED)

Height of Shrub* (in.)	Size of Pit (Diameter)
18/24"	16 × 10" (40.64 × 25.40 cm)
24/36"	18 × 12" (45.72 × 30.48 cm)
36/48"	20 × 14" (50.8 × 35.56 cm)

Caliper of Tree*	Size of Pit (Diameter)
1 −1½"	34 × 21" (86.36 × 53.34 cm)
1½−2"	36 × 22" (91.44 × 55.88 cm)
2 −2½"	40 × 25" (101.6 × 63.5 cm)
2½−3"	44 × 26" (111.76 × 66.04 cm)
3 −4"	52 × 30" (132.08 × 76.2 cm)
4 −5"	56 × 32" (142.24 × 81.28 cm)

To determine pit volume in cubic feet: (3.14) (diameter in inches^2) ÷ 4 × depth in inches × 1,728 = volume

*Horticultural Determination

CONTAINER STOCK — VOLUME OF SOIL

Size (Gal.)	Vol. (Ft.³)
1	0.13
2	0.27
5	0.67
7	0.94

GROUND COVER PLANTING

Spacing of Plants	Multiplier
4" (10.16 cm) on center	9.1
6" (15.24 cm) o.c.	4
9" (22.86 cm) o.c.	1.77
12" (30.48 cm) o.c.	1
18" (45.72 cm) o.c.	.45
24" (60.96 cm) o.c.	.25

(Square feet of planting area × multiplier = number of plants required)

PLANTING BALL VOLUMES AND WEIGHTS

Ball Size	Volume (cu. ft.)	Weight* (lbs.)
18 × 14″	1.81	155–200
20 × 15″	2.39	203–263
22 × 15″	2.89	246–318
24 × 16″	2.64	310–400
28 × 18″	5.62	477–618
32 × 20″	9.30	741–1023
38 × 22″	14.43	1111–1587
42 × 27″	12.95	1610–2084
46 × 28″	26.92	2218–2691
54 × 33″	38.20	3255–4210

Volume of planting ball = (ball diameter in feet)^2 × ball depth in feet × ⅔

*Weight range depending on soil density

PLANTING CONTAINER VOLUMES AND WEIGHTS

Container Size (Gal.)	Vol. (cu. ft.)	Weight (lbs.)
1	.13	12–14
2	.27	24–29
5	.67	60–73
7	.94	85–103

CONVERSION FACTORS

1 inch	= 2.54 centimeters	1 centimeter	= .3937 inch
1 foot	= .3048 meter	1 decimeter	= .3281 foot
1 yard	= .9144 meter	1 meter	= 1.094 yards
1 kilometer	= .6214 mile	1 mile	= 1.609 kilometers
1 sq. inch	= 6.452 sq. centimeters	1 sq. yard	= 0.836 sq. meter
1 sq. foot	= .093 sq. meter	1 sq. mile	= 2.590 sq. kilometers

Cubic Measure:

1 cu. foot	= 1,728 cu. inches
	= 0.037 cu. yards
	= 7.48 gallons
	= 28.32 liters
1 cu. yard	= 27 cu. feet
	= 46,656 cu. inches
	= 202 gallons

To convert cubic feet to gallons:

cubic feet × 7.48

To convert gallons to cubic feet:

gallons × 0.1337

Square Measure:

1 sq. foot	= 144 sq. inches
1 sq. yard	= 1,296 sq. inches
	= 9 sq. feet
1 sq. mile	= 640 acres
1 acre	= 43,560 sq. feet
	= 4,840 sq. yards

Angular Measure:

60 seconds	= 1 minute
60 minutes	= 1 degree
360 degrees	= 1 circle
60 degrees	= 1 sextant
90 degrees	= 1 quadrant

CONCRETE REINFORCING BARS — STANDARD SIZES

Bar No.	Diameter
2	¼″ (0.635 cm)
3	⅜″ (0.952 cm)
4	½″ (1.27 cm)
5	⅝″ (1.59 cm)
6	¾″ (1.90 cm)
7	⅞″ (2.22 cm)
8	1″ (2.54 cm)

PLANTS PER LINEAR FOOT OF HEDGE (ESTIMATE)

Plant Spacing	Plants Per Lineal Foot	Plants Per 10 Lineal Feet
10″ (25.40 cm)	1.2	12.0
12″ (30.48 cm)	1.0	10.0
15″ (38.10 cm)	.8	8.0
18″ (45.72 cm)	.67	6.7
24″ (60.96 cm)	.5	5.0
30″ (76.20 cm)	.4	4.0
3′ (0.91 m)	.33	3.3
4′ (1.22 m)	.25	2.5
5′ (1.53 m)	.2	2.0

MINIMUM GRADES FOR SURFACE DRAINAGE

Use	Ratio—Horizontal to Vertical	Percentage
Patio	1″(2.54cm) in 10′(3.05m)	(.8% slope)
Open lawn— well-drained	1″(2.54cm) in 8′(2.44m)	(1% slope)
Open lawn— heavy soil	1″(2.54cm) in 4′(1.22m)	(2% slope)
Around building foundations and areas required good drainage	1″(2.54cm) in 2′(0.61m)	(5% slope)

TREE AND SHRUB PLANTING REQUIREMENTS—TIME FACTORS

1. Staking out plants = 25/hour
2. Dig planting pit, average soil = 20 cu. feet/hour
3. Place tree in planting pit

(Weight of plant, lbs.)	# per hour
50–100	12.5
100–200	12.5
200–300	6.25
300–400	4.37
400–500	3.12

4. Backfill planting pit, average soil = 28.75 cu. ft./hour
5. Prune tree of dead or injured wood:

Size (caliper)	# per hour
1″	11.87
2″	6.25
over 2″	5.25

6. Prune shrubs of dead or injured wood:

Size (height)	# per hour
to 3'	24.37
3–6'	11.87
over 6'	6.25

7. Wrapping tree with burlap:

Size (caliper)	# per hour
1"–2"	18.75
2"–4"	6.25
4"–6"	4.37

8. Guying tree (three wooden stakes):

Size (caliper)	# per hour
up to 3"	3.12
3"–6"	1.75
6" and up	1.12

9. Planting ground cover plants:

Size of Pot	# per hour
2¼"	75
3"	50
4"	35

10. Planting container plants:

Size	# per hour
1 quart	12.5
1 gallon	7.5
2 gallon	5.6
5 gallon	3.1

11. Lawn sodding:

Function	
hand-place sod	438.75 sq. feet
roll sod w/hand roller	3,999.28 sq. feet

12. Soil tilling

Depth of till	Area per hour
4" (by hand)	67.5 sq. feet

6″ (by hand)	50.63 sq. feet
4″ (w/rototiller)	798.75 sq. feet
6″ (w/rototiller)	601.87 sq. feet

13. Lawn seeding:

Function	Area per hour
hand broadcast	0.201 acres
push spreader	0.459 acres
800 gal. hydroseeder	1.799 acres
1,500 gal. hydroseeder	4.65 acres

14. Lawn mowing:

Equipment	Minutes per 1,000 ft.²
25″ power motor	3
58″ power motor	1
7′ power motor	½

15. Edge and trim:

Operation	Minutes per 100 linear feet
hand trim along walks	25−30
power trimmer	8−10
around shrubs	
by hand	45−60
power trimmer	30−40

(All figures regarding time are averaged for semi-skilled laborers working an eight-hour day in medium soils.)

180

APPENDIX 4

IMPLEMENTATION DETAILS

The following are typical planting-plan implementation details that are useful in communicating required planting requirements:

    A. Typical tree planting detail
    B. Small shrub, groundcover, or annual flowers in pots/gravel
    C. Typical shrub-planting detail
    D. Typical tree planting with guy wires
    E. Tree planting on berm
    F. Small tree/large shrub bracing
    G. Tree-planting detail under concrete pavers
    H. Large tree bracing
    I. Tree-planting detail, brick pavers on sand

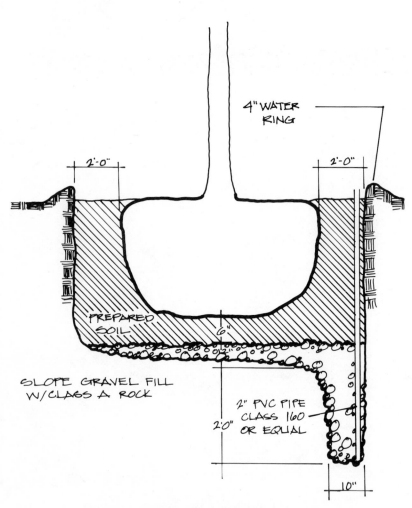

4" WATER RING

2'-0"   2'-0"

PREPARED SOIL

6"

12"

SLOPE GRAVEL FILL W/CLASS A ROCK

2'0"

2" PVC PIPE CLASS 160 OR EQUAL

10"

DETAIL-TREE PLANTING

A

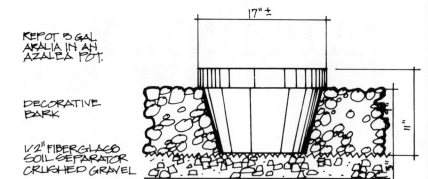

REPOT 5 GAL ARALIA IN AN AZALEA POT.

DECORATIVE BARK

1/2" FIBERGLASS SOIL SEPARATOR CRUSHED GRAVEL

17" ±

11"

3"

PLANTING DETAIL FOR ARALIA SIEBOLDI
SCALE: 1-1/2"=1'-0"

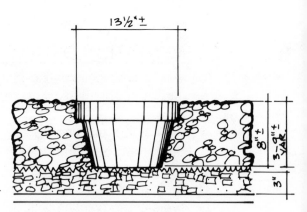

REPOT 2 GAL. FATSHEDRA & 8"POT HAHN'S IVY IN AZALEA POT.

DECORATIVE BARK VARIES IN DEPTH.

1/2" FIBERGLASS SOIL SEPARATOR CRUSHED GRAVEL

13 1/2" ±

8" ±

3"-9" ± VARIES

3"

PLANTING DETAIL FOR FATSHEDRA & HAHN'S IVY
SCALE: 1 1/2"=1'-0"

B

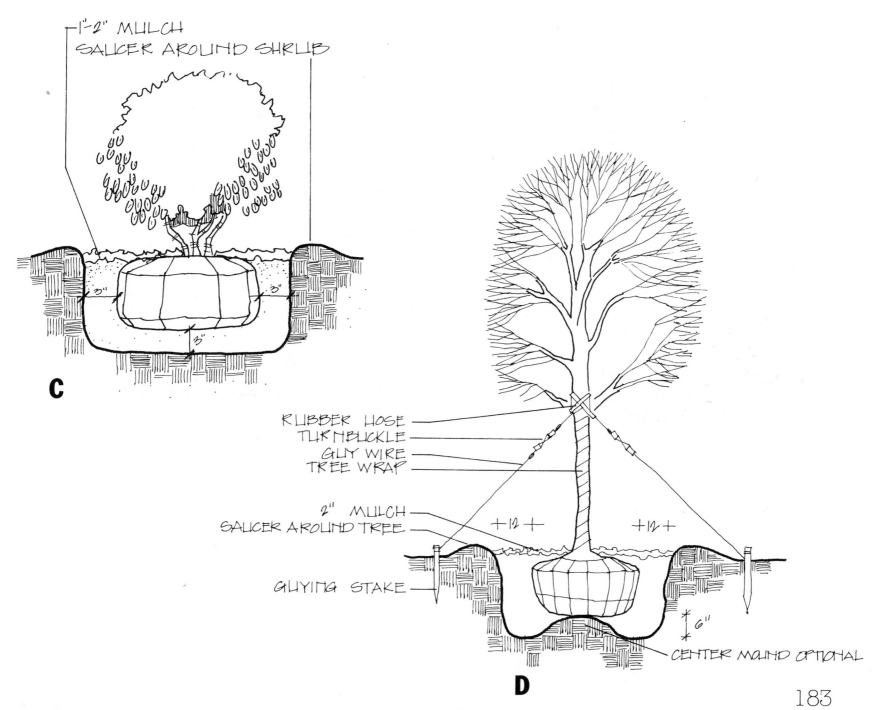

SHRUB PLANTING:

1"-2" MULCH
SALICER AROUND SHRUB

3"
3"
3"

C

RUBBER HOSE
TURNBUCKLE
GUY WIRE
TREE WRAP

2" MULCH
SALICER AROUND TREE

+12+   +12+

GUYING STAKE

6"

CENTER MOUND OPTIONAL

D

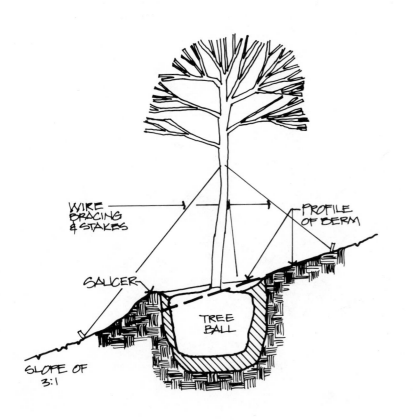

WIRE BRACING & STAKES

PROFILE OF BERM

SALICER

TREE BALL

SLOPE OF 3:1

TREE PLANTING ON BERM

E

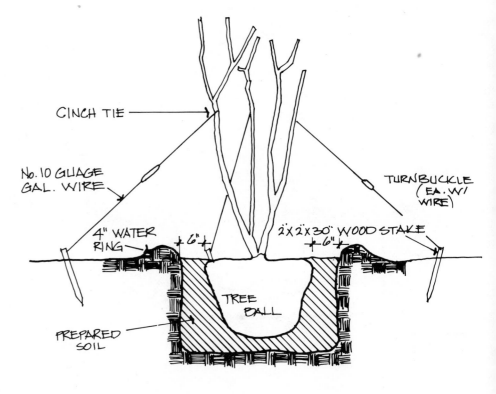

CINCH TIE

No. 10 GUAGE GAL. WIRE

TURNBUCKLE (EA. W/ WIRE)

4" WATER RING

6"

2"X 2"X 30" WOOD STAKE

6"

TREE BALL

PREPARED SOIL

DETAIL - SMALL TREE BRACING

F

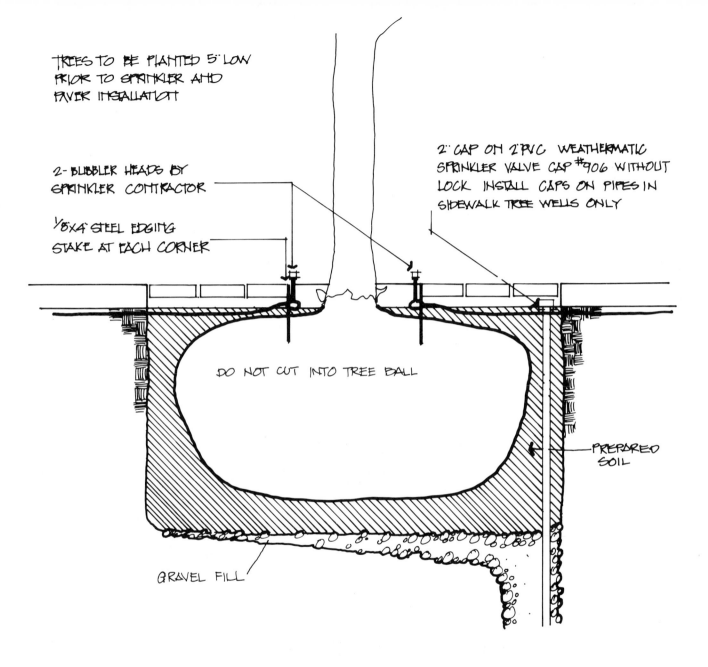

TREES TO BE PLANTED 5" LOW
PRIOR TO SPRINKLER AND
PAVER INSTALLATION

2-BUBBLER HEADS BY
SPRINKLER CONTRACTOR

1/8 X 4" STEEL EDGING
STAKE AT EACH CORNER

2" CAP ON 2" PVC WEATHERMATIC
SPRINKLER VALVE CAP #906 WITHOUT
LOCK INSTALL CAPS ON PIPES IN
SIDEWALK TREE WELLS ONLY

DO NOT CUT INTO TREE BALL

PREPARED SOIL

GRAVEL FILL

SECTION-TREE PLANTING DETAIL

G

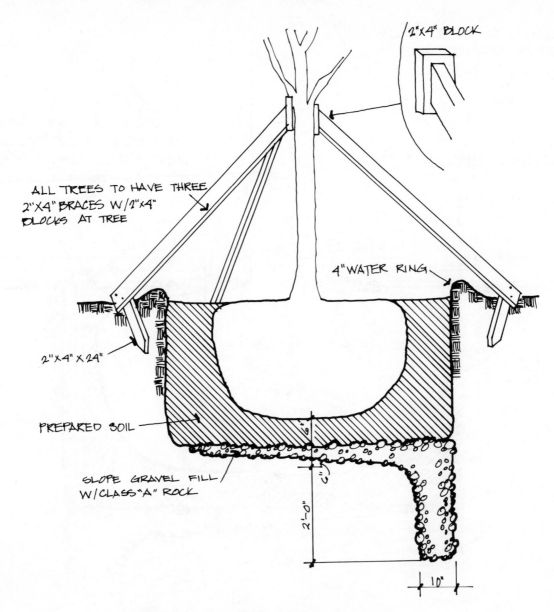

2"X4" BLOCK

ALL TREES TO HAVE THREE
2"X4" BRACES W/2"X4"
BLOCKS AT TREE

4"WATER RING

2"X4" X 24"

PREPARED SOIL

SLOPE GRAVEL FILL
W/CLASS "A" ROCK

6"

2'-0"

10"

DETAIL - LARGE TREE BRACING

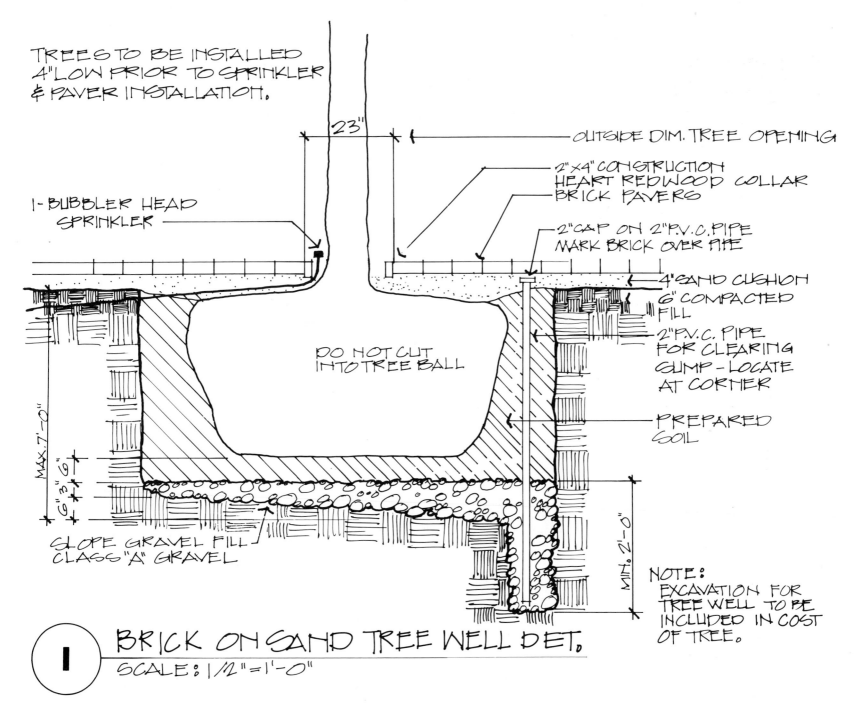

TREES TO BE INSTALLED 4" LOW PRIOR TO SPRINKLER & PAVER INSTALLATION.

23"

OUTSIDE DIM. TREE OPENING

1- BUBBLER HEAD SPRINKLER

2"x4" CONSTRUCTION HEART REDWOOD COLLAR

BRICK PAVERS

2" CAP ON 2" P.V.C. PIPE MARK BRICK OVER PIPE

DO NOT CUT INTO TREE BALL

4" SAND CUSHION

6" COMPACTED FILL

2" P.V.C. PIPE FOR CLEARING SUMP - LOCATE AT CORNER

PREPARED SOIL

Max. 7'-0"

6" 3" 6"

SLOPE GRAVEL FILL CLASS "A" GRAVEL

MIN. 2'-0"

NOTE:
EXCAVATION FOR TREE WELL TO BE INCLUDED IN COST OF TREE.

① BRICK ON SAND TREE WELL DET.
SCALE: 1/2" = 1'-0"

187

INDEX